The Soccer Hutch

Soccer knowledge for the local-level game

Paul Hutchinson

ISBN-10: 1475073070
ISBN-13: 978-1475073072

Contents

Introduction

Soccer has been played with the same number of players, on the same sized pitches and under more or less the same rules for over 100 years. There are thousands and thousands of games at various levels each week.

Incidents that happen in any given week, on any pitch, may appear random and exclusive to that very match.

They are, in fact, very rarely random and are usually variations on a theme. Give or take the colour of a shirt or other irrelevant details, the same pattern of play, incident or goal is probably happening somewhere else, in another match, at the very same time.

Such is the rigidity of the systems and tactics, and the homogeneous nature of players, teams, pitches and soccer balls that even the most bizarre of own-goals, deflections or passages of play are likely to happen again — and soon — in another game.

When you discount the bizarre, the standard passages of play leading to typical goals are extremely frequent occurrences. So much so, they can be premeditated and staged on a regular basis. Like a chess move, they can be documented.

You just have to hope the opponent plays his prescribed acquiescent role in the action.

I have played or managed every season, in adult local-level soccer leagues, for 35 years, whilst living and working in six different countries: England, Spain, Germany, Holland, Hong Kong and Ireland.

This is my analysis of the local lower-league game. How it works and how it should work. I hope to capture some of the philosophy behind team shape and positional play that consistently leads to the situations we see in every game of soccer.

It is an attempt to document a way of setting out a team and a style of play that creates more positive frequently occurring moments than negative ones.

I hope to take some basics of soccer knowledge and present them in a way that ties all aspects of the lower-league team's game together.

The professional game can maintain and build on the knowledge and theory of soccer, passing it on successfully through the ranks, and enhancing it through the years.

Unless professionally taught, (debatably innate in gifted individuals), soccer knowledge slowly infuses, through experience.

The experience of hours spent playing, watching and contemplating the game.

Eventually the patterns emerge and its basic, beautiful simplicity is revealed.

I presume to have some knowledge. I had only glimpses of that knowledge when I was playing at my peak of physical ability.

I want to record that purported knowledge. Unlike the professional game, at lower local-league level, we have nobody contracted to us, nobody to pass it on to.

In lower non-league, soccer knowledge runs through our fingers like grains of sand. Every season, experienced players leave the game just when they are beginning to understand it, to focus on individual sports, family or career pursuits.

The learning process begins again, with new players forced to learn it slowly, through their own experience.

They rarely have the advantage of tapping into another's previous and similar experience.

At local level, the team learning curve never shortens.

Many good local-level players do not stick long enough at the adult game to gain an adequate knowledge of soccer. Their knowledge needs to be fast-tracked.

If I can write my version of it down simply and effectively enough, maybe I can share it with others, or at least record its existence for my own purpose, before I also move on.

This book aims at those involved in lower local and "expenses paid" soccer. It states the obvious and in certain chapters, contains simplifications, contradictions and repetition. All, I hope, necessary coaching tools.

Soccer is a simple game.

It is not so simple to portray in print or to convert from the printed theory into practice.

Despite the opening paragraphs, it is also beautifully random. Bizarre incidents and goals happen, week-in, week-out. Luck plays a major part. No coach or player can prepare for that.

He can prepare for the expected.

Soccer knowledge is not everything. If it were, it would be a game for old men. They would spread play around, letting the ball do the work, albeit in slow motion.

Physical ability, with the basic understanding, beats full knowledge at half pace every time. That is why good soccer is an athletic, young person's game. It is a running sport.

Soccer is an individual and a team game. The hugely important *individual* side of the team game is harder to define. Suffice to say we can all spot a good player and it pays to have one in your side.

A good player with ability, imagination and spontaneity, unconsciously utilising soccer theory within an organised team structure, makes all the difference.

Good players employ the theory without giving it a second thought. If you had to think of it, you would not be able to do it in time. This theory can be recorded.

This book is concerned with the team aspect of local lower-league soccer. It seeks to promote your thoughts on, and encourage use of, the pass-and-move game as it relates to the lower-league levels.

Ours should be a slower version of the professional game, not the very different game we have. Our team shape is impaired, on and off the pitch. As a result, from first principles, doing the right thing is more difficult.

I hope the chapters stand alone but also interact, just as they have to in the game of soccer.

Imparting soccer knowledge to a team is a complex matter. To do so through mental visualisation via reading a book is a tall order. Maybe for some, there is no substitute for going through the complete practical learning process themselves.

I still think there are corners that can be cut; and access to parts of the sterile theory, even in print, can open the mind and stimulate improvement.

I hope you will be able to visualise the written word as an on-the-pitch moment. I believe, "**if you can see it in your mind, you can do it on the pitch**".

This book, like good soccer, relies heavily on that concept.

Note: Individual non-specific persons in the book are often referred to using "he", "him", or "his". This should be taken to mean "she" etc. as appropriate.

1

Team Shape

One of the fundamental concepts in football is keeping your shape. If there were one thing that a technical coach could do in local football to improve the way a team might play, it would be to insist on **the correct team shape in ball possession**.

Shape is all-important. The ball moves through this team structure. The structure connects one player's task with another's and forms organised units of them. Without the **correct starting shape**, a team cannot begin to realise many of the passing and collective movements that lead to goals.

Many local teams play as if 4-4-2 was just a way of writing the names on the team sheet.

Whatever the formation, it is of course the shape of the team on the pitch and in particular when in *safe midfield or defensive possession of the ball*.

In local parks, you often hear a manager or captain shout, "let's get our shape".

What normally happens then is that everybody squeezes onto the opposition to show that they have their man marked.

They are concerned with "our shape" *when the opponents have the ball*.

If anything separates a local game from the paid variety, it would be the shape the teams adopt on the pitch, not to mention the physical shape of some of the players.

You only need to look at the positions of both sets of players during open play to be able to tell what standard of game you are watching.

If you watch a professional game, let us say 4-4-2 with the ball in open play around the centre circle, the team *without* the ball will have two parallel, defensive lines of four players, spread out, *covering the pitch* from wing to wing.

This is the right defensive shape and *arises in direct response* to the right attacking shape.

Moreover, if we **get the team shape right in possession**, it will adapt quickly to a sudden ball loss. For if the team is in the right shape in possession, it will have one or two players available in each area if the move breaks down.

The one or two players who were offering support to the area where the ball was lost must now hold up the opposition attack until players who committed to a forward run can come back. They come back in units, as well as go forward in units. They get behind the ball before they help squeeze it.

If we get the shape in possession correct, the shape in defence should naturally follow.

The right attacking shape or shape in possession dictates that the team with the ball has both its wingers and full backs **maintaining their width** regardless of which side of the pitch the ball might be on.

Both sides know they have the quality to switch play from one wing to the other in an instant and so they must have players already out there, available when that switch comes.

By maintaining their width and **pushing up on both sides**, they have created space in the middle of the pitch to allow the midfielders a chance to get their heads up and play.

The central midfield is the fulcrum of any team.

It is the hub and if your players can get the ball under control here and distribute the ball throughout the shape, you have started to play football.

The centre halves of the team in possession help to **create space for the midfield**. They drop off from the opposing attackers. They offer a backward safe-pass alternative to the midfielder who can recycle a move through them.

This creates an arched shape at the back with the full backs hugging the touchlines and pushing up to just within the opposition half; and the centre halves backing off to deep within their own half.

Just as the centre halves back off, stretching the defensive arc one way, the strikers, wingers and attacking midfielder push up, forcing the opposition back to cover their movements.

This space creation at both ends of the pitch gives the team shape that is necessary if the ball is to be circulated through it.

The two centre halves **act as a possession safety net**, positioned at least 25 yards apart. They can play to each other and to either full back, using the central midfielders, especially the holding one as a link. They therefore not only provide an out-ball to maintain possession, but can switch play quickly to either side.

Therefore, the basic attacking shape of a good team in possession on the centre line is an **arc for the back line and an arc for the midfield line**.

This midfield arc contorts as the ball hits the attacking last third, with the attacking midfielder moving forward to create a diamond effect as the holding midfielder remains to link play.

The two central midfielders and one of the two forwards, being central, have the job of fetch, carry and feed for the wide players, allowing them to stay wide, with the eventual aim of getting as many attacking players as possible into the attacking last third, with the ball under control.

The more attacking players in that last third, the greater the chance of creating one of the three ways to score. See chapter 3, *Scoring a Goal*. You particularly want width in this attacking last third, as crosses offer the most likely way of scoring goals.

This is the shape of good modern football. The bad news is that this shape is only achieved and sustained through good movement and crisp passing. See chapter 2, *Pass and Move*.

In the **typical shape of local soccer**, where the focus is often on keeping pressure on your opposite number at all times, you will rarely see the arched shape in possession. Consequently, it is rare that a player *gets time in midfield* to lift up his head and play.

The main reason for this is not that the opposition puts pressure on in numbers when your midfielder has the ball. *This can be dealt with*. It is more that his own team's players have not kept their shape and width and have therefore not created space for him.

In fact, they have put pressure on him themselves by *coming in too close*, in a misguided attempt to help him out.

Each member of the team who squeezes his own midfielder on the ball usually brings one of the opposition with him. This results in a congregation of local footballers immediately around the ball. The level of football played is betrayed in a snapshot by the *compressed shape* of the teams on the pitch.

In this situation, even if the midfielder does get his head up with the ball under control, his options are now limited. Since his own teammates have come into his area bringing their opposite members, they become his focus for a successful pass.

The number of opposition and teammates now in the midfield area *narrows the angles and shortens the distance of the passes*, making the risk of losing the ball very high.

The midfielder does not have the option of the pass out wide if the winger has come inside "to help". Even if he does pass it to the winger, this winger is now not in a much better position than the midfielder.

Most local wingers and full backs do not **hug the touchline in possession**, even if play looks to be coming to their side.

When the ball is on their flank, the winger is seldom given **space to play** but is joined up close by his central midfielders, full back and a forward.

In squeezing their own winger, they squeeze the life out of his attacking options. It is **the opponent's job to squeeze him**, not yours.

In fact, the winger on the opposite side of play, keen to get involved, often comes over even further than the centre of the pitch.

You do not have width just because you have the ball on the wing.

If your team squeezes over towards that wing, you have narrowness.

You will only have width if the other wing also contains teammates, thus **stretching the pitch and creating space** all across the pitch.

The centre halves of the team in possession do not drop back away from their midfield and create the arc. By not **backing away to provide a safe out pass**, they push the opposing forward they are marking into the midfield area, providing yet another threat to their own midfielder in possession and further compacting the game.

What, of course, the centre halves should do is drop off and **create the arc in possession**.

They should be available as an out pass, keeping an eye on their opposition forwards but only squeezing on to them, giving the **flat defensive line of four**, the instant possession is lost.

The result is often all 20 outfield players on one side of the pitch with no definable shape, either with or without possession.

Not keeping the shape leads to all sorts of problems in the local game, especially and ironically if a team tries to play a passing football game without the correct shape.

In each local team, there is usually at least one or two who try in vain to play a pass-and-move game.

Without the right shape, or in its place **exceptional short passing and movement**, there is no structure through which the ball can safely flow.

These one or two players will end up passing their own team into trouble and will bear the brunt of the criticism when possession is lost in midfield areas.

The hub of the game is too crowded and keeping possession within it, without safe wide and safe backward *out* passes, is very difficult.

The *big switch* is no longer possible if the wingers and full backs have deemed it necessary to *tuck in* when the play is on the opposite side.

Drop a playmaker-type, professional-level player into this midfield and he would find it difficult to maintain possession without ordering his teammates to adopt the right positions and shape. A task that in local football is easier said than done.

A lot can be learned about the *crucial importance of shape* by considering how a rugby team operates.

The **players have to keep their shape** and create such a connecting line of players that the ball can be run from one end of the pitch to the other, being passed backwards quickly.

If they tried to create this line only after gathering possession, they would never be able to run quick enough to get into position to receive the ball.

The fact is *the ball can move quicker than a player ever will* and so the shape needs to be there first, *followed by the ball.*

There are aspects of the vicious circle, chicken-and-egg and self-fulfilling prophecy; all involved in the reasons why low-level soccer teams do not or cannot copy the shape of the professional teams in possession.

The right way to do it **is simple**. The wrong way is quite complicated.

Rather than the centre halves dropping off and creating the **necessary arc shape**, they continue pretty much, non-stop, to mark their forward.

They expect their own midfield or forwards to turn over possession almost immediately and so they will make sure their man is more or less permanently marked.

Of course, this means that they follow and squeeze the opposing forward into their own midfielders and thereby increase the likelihood that the opposition will tackle the midfielder.

It also ensures that they rarely **offer a safe backward out pass** to the midfielder, again condemning him in certain situations to concede possession.

Worse still, not only does the centre half continue to mark his forward when his team has possession, but depending on which side of the pitch the ball is, he often pulls a full back in to help him.

Thus removing another *possible safe out-pass* for a midfielder in possession.

The midfielder, embattled as he is by the numbers now in his area, will often contribute to his own problems. I often hear shouts of, "they've three in the middle" and suddenly the central midfielder has called a winger in, supposedly to help him.

In the event of the midfielder actually getting possession, he has now deprived himself of a possible safe out-pass to the wing, as the wing is now minus its winger.

If the ball is on the left-hand side of the pitch, the right-winger will very often decide of his own accord to come inside to try to get in on the action.

The opponents then cover this move, which may bring in yet another member of our team, again supposedly to help. The ball moves out of that area, the teams briefly expand their game only to tighten right up again, around the ball, in a different area of the pitch.

There you have the typical evolution of the shape in possession of a lower league team. Each squeeze of the opposition, instead of being countered by an expansion, encourages a squeeze from your own team. The effect for ball maintenance is fatal.

Due to the compressed shape of the lower league team in possession, many passes go astray in the clogged midfield.

The manager and the leaders on the pitch, who are very often in the spine of the team, particularly at the back, realise that losing the ball like this in midfield is putting them under constant sudden pressure in defence.

The answer selected to solve this problem, like many solutions to life's problems, is short term, superficial and ultimately ineffective.

The fault is identified as "playing football at the back and midfield is killing us". Hence, the sentiment of not being good enough to play football in those areas.

Ultimately, players are selected whose attributes best match this long ball, low risk, high *ball turnover* game. This helps perpetuate the system, as more technically gifted or pass-oriented players are considered a luxury or a risk.

That type of player is considered too lightweight for the robust nature of this lower league style.

The preferred player is somebody who can physically compete in the numerous 50/50 loose-ball situations.

Somebody who can run between defence and attack in endless pursuit of the ball.

A player who is *not* looking to **pass it square or backwards**, in his own half.

The players at the back are now encouraged to bypass midfield and put the ball up towards the forwards at each opportunity. The midfield is urged not to pass square or back but also to put the ball forward at every opportunity.

Now the ball is being lost even more than before, but in a position perceived as less dangerous, i.e. further up the pitch and in the opponent's half.

This *apparently* works better as the back four now have periods of relief whilst the ball is in their opposition's half, rather than the constant alert they were under whilst the ball was being passed short in midfield.

A high offside line is a by-product of squeezing up onto the forwards at all times. This leads to many calls for offside and is a constant danger for the lower league defence.

Fortunately for the defenders in many low-level games, there are no referee assistants available or they are inexperienced and flag-happy. So the referee tends to whistle in favour of the defence in all but the most obvious cases of onside.

To be fair to the local-level referee, getting it right with or without a linesman in light of the new non-interference law is not easy. If in doubt, siding with the defence is often the less stressful route. See chapter 16, *Referees*.

The two wingers are now centre midfield players, playing just a bit wider, as they rarely receive the ball on the wing in space enough to behave like wingers.

They are tucked in, busy marking their opposite number who is busy tucking in, marking them.

The full backs are also too busy tucking in, helping the centre half, rather than marking wingers, especially those that do not play on the wing.

The two centre midfielders are now hammering up and down the pitch, trying to help their centre halves and their forwards deal with the constant stream of long balls dropping into them.

The forwards now compete with four defenders for constant long passes from the back and hurried hopeful passes from midfield.

This, on top of the many clearances and long passes, which they have to deal with, as a normal part of the game of soccer.

Their chance of holding on to the ball under these conditions is reduced by the lack of support from midfield, despite best efforts to reach them.

The lack of **build-up play** seldom gives the midfield adequate time to move up front and join in with their strikers.

A pass-and-move system is only possible within the correct team shape in possession.

Both sides therefore turn over the ball regularly, as their lack of a pass-and-move system to outwit each other and maintain possession leaves a stalemate.

This stalemate determines that the result will normally be decided by whichever team has the best individuals winning individual battles, rather than the best team game.

With this stalemate, the circle of the game of football is as complete at local level as it often is in the professional game.

Individual talent is the remedy chosen to break the stalemate.

In the professional game, where all teams apply the basic theory of pass-and-move and keep their arched shape in possession, a certain stalemate can arise.

It can be a stalemate of too many passes rather than too few, as in the lower level.

Unless you are protecting a lead and playing keep ball, passing is not an objective in itself.

Passing the ball is intended eventually to find a gap in the opposition, to find a weakness where an opponent, mesmerised by the **seemingly innocuous passes**, loses his concentration long enough for a killer pass to be delivered.

If the passing and movement is not quick or expert enough, the passes do become *innocuous*. Defending against a slow "pass-and-move" game for a professionally fit team becomes easy.

The opposition matches the basics of *keeping shape and pass-and-move* and now a better, quicker pass-and-move game is necessary if you are to have a superior team game.

This means educating the players to play a **better, quicker, pass-and-move game** and requires a brave footballing manager with a longer-term vision. I was going to write longer-term contract, but it does not appear they are worth the paper they are written on in the professional game.

The normal, easier, quicker and temporary solution (if you have the cash) is to get better individuals to give your side the individual edge over other teams.

Alternatively, through your man management and player assessment skills, you blend less-valued individuals to bring out a heightened individual performance from each other.

Thus, the professionals, just as the lower local-league teams, become dependent on having better individuals than the opposition to provide the competitive advantage on an individual basis.

The transfer market for the best individual footballers in the world, in what is **a team game**, would confirm this. The better teams add the superior individual to an already superior team game. Others just add the superior individuals.

Inferior professional opposition, rather like a local league side, may try to pack central areas and their own attacking team shape suffers.

They may concede the bulk of possession, but are happy to do so.

The difference being that professional footballers, that much fitter on the same size pitches, make a better job of stifling play, protecting their goal, winning the ball and making the most of the random opportunities this style of play brings.

They **expand out into the correct attacking shape** upon winning the ball much quicker than would be possible with the fitness and speed of local-level players.

Professional teams squeeze and expand in a more exaggerated fashion. At a lower level, it is better to keep your shape, keeping a bit of width available, as we are not quick enough or fit enough, nor do we keep the ball long enough, to expand effectively with it.

In the lower leagues, most teams seem happy enough with the reality of the compressed nature of their game. It is easier to find individuals whose style suits the compacted shape and bring an individual advantage rather than change the team's mentality from an individual to a team one.

Fortunately, the opposition is just as caught up in this lower-league mentality.

So a pass-and-move style of play is made first possible by the team shape.

The local game, due to its lack of the correct shape in possession, is condemned to frequent ball loss and few consecutive passes, with games settled in the main by superior individual performances.

The correct shape in possession must come first.

The individuals must first do the basics of keeping their shape and then apply any physical or technical advantage they have within the confines and the freedoms provided by the shape.

Individual play as an advantage should be sought as the icing on the cake.

When the basics of pass-and-move have successfully been applied through the structure of the shape, an individual should seek to pursue any advantage he has over his opposition, in whichever guise it comes, whether in **strength, speed, technical ability, physical stature and agility** or mentally through **cleverness and experience**.

When you watch good football, you will see little *pockets of activity* in small areas of the pitch whilst other areas look almost static. The correct shape distorts slightly with this movement.

The opponents squeeze the ball and the unit in possession is forced to tighten up to protect it and enable the switch to a less pressured area of *the correct shape*.

The activity and distortion changes from area to area as the ball moves through or between the arcs, engaging different units of players.

How to make local players adopt the correct shape in possession?

Trying to improve the standard of play and thus fixing a team's shape first is hindered by the all-consuming desire for a result from every game. From the pros down to the under-elevens, the desire *not to lose* gets in the way of the beautiful game.

As often in life, the long-term goal loses out to the short term.

As a manager, you have to show the courage of your convictions to improve the playing standard and insist, number one, on maintaining the correct shape.

You will come under pressure from many sources to let the players do it the way they always do it. You will need to stand up to this.

The centre halves will not be happy dropping off their attackers when we have the ball. They will not want to put their foot on the ball, get their heads up and play football at the back. They will consider this risky and will not at first see the reward.

They will want to pull a full back in to help them in most situations, when the correct shape would dictate that the full back remains free, out wide.

The manager must insist that **the centre halves drop off and provide the arc shape** for their midfielders. They must *not* play a high line in possession and they should *not* be afraid to get on the ball around the outside of their 18-yard box.

They outnumber the opponents here and must take the responsibility of being actively involved in the pass-and-move game. The two centre halves **should not get too close**, 15-35 yards, if they are to offer a safe out pass for each other.

They each should make sure the one on the ball has an option, even if one centre half has to drop back to offer it. **The man on the ball should not be the last man**, unless he has a definite, safe option to pass the ball or is clearing it.

The centre halves must be encouraged in their decision-making: when to pass or keep the ball and when to clear it up to the forwards.

Only they can make the right decision and the quality of football, like the quality of life, depends on the decisions we make.

Decision-making can be the difference between a good and a bad player and it's often the team which makes the fewest bad decisions that comes off best.

The manager must insist that **the full back only comes inside to help when the opposition is in possession and moving up into our defensive last third**. Protecting the goal now takes precedence over providing a safe out.

The midfielders may complain that they are outnumbered in the middle as the opposition continues to squeeze in number in the central positions.

A midfielder may call a winger into the middle to help.

The manager must insist that the two central midfielders maintain a central position. They should not get too close to each other (10-30 yards).

They need room to pass to each other and to make the distances and angles large enough so that one opposition player cannot close them both down, in seconds.

The **distances that players maintain from each other in possession** should, as a rule, be the maximum possible *whilst still providing a safe pass*.

Too close and the player will be instantly closed down and any territorial gain from the pass is minimal. Too far apart and the pass may be intercepted or its difficulty unnecessarily severe.

The central midfielders' new role is as *the hub*. It is their job to distribute the ball to all areas of the pitch and to provide a link from one area of *the correct shape* to another.

They should endeavour to get the ball out wide to the full backs and the wingers.

They must **keep their wingers and full backs out wide and available** to stretch the game and receive a pass.

The opposition's extra numbers in the central area will become a liability to them if your team successfully moves the ball out of the congested area to the wings.

It takes a while for a team to learn a new shape, depending on the quality of the players. It may not suit all.

However, you get out of it what you put into it and you must fully commit to the new "correct shape in possession" for it to work.

You cannot pick bits of it and expect to be able to play a pass-and-move game.

There are many different shapes that the team adopts during a game. These are **starting shapes** from which runs are made that distort the shape but progress the move.

There is a **correct shape for all dead-ball situations**, especially your own ones. You must adopt these correct shapes so that you are in position to make the correct timed runs. See the chapters on throw-ins, corners and free kicks.

A good chance to get your team shape correct is at your own goal kick. Have the two centre halves take up a position 30 yards apart and 10 yards outside the corner edges of the 18-yard box.

The two full backs go wide 25 yards further up, creating the curved line of a team in possession. The wingers also hang wide and further up from the two central midfielders.

The attacking midfielder also pushes on, taking his opponent away with him and creating space around your box.

The centre forwards push the defence back as far as possible, whilst remaining onside for any second-ball or flick-on. You cannot be offside directly from a goal kick.

You now have the correct shape of a team in possession, with two curved lines of four ready to deal with the ball if it falls to your team.

You have also created a space for your forwards and midfielders to compete for the ball and deal with it, as it lands from the goal kick.

When the long goal kick is taken, the centre halves follow it out at half pace, watching it go over their heads and reading the resulting situation as the ball drops. Any forward who stood with them is now following the ball out as well or risking being off side.

If the opposition forwards do not mark or hang around the centre halves, they can even quickly drop back and receive the ball from the kick and are in the correct shape to start a possession move up the pitch. See the pass-and-move chapter for this scenario.

If the long goal kick is taken, they are now in a good position to deal with any headed ball won by the opposing defence and knocked forward towards them.

They are moving towards it with a little momentum and don't have to turn and chase it. They have their opposition forwards also retreating and in their eye-line.

If the ball is won, the shape is perfect for maintaining possession. If the ball is lost, then they and the rest of their teammates **quickly squeeze onto their relevant man**, flattening the curved lines of midfield and defence.

At the first intercepted square pass in midfield or the first centre half closed down, there will be cries to return to clearing it at all times in your own half and marking the opposition at all times, in case of sudden ball loss.

If you succumb to the pressure and abandon the attempt to insist on *the correct shape* you will again see your football matches decided on the individual superiority of players over other players in certain positions.

Unless your team is lucky enough to have a steady stream of superior individuals, the best long-term policy would be to adopt a superior playing style.

In local teams, the quality is always going to be of a level. Superior individual players, if on their way up, will not stay with you long. The chances of your local team laying claim to better players than other local teams in the same standard leagues are low.

You should choose to **compete on fitness, playing style and tactics**. At the lower levels, there is huge scope to compete successfully through these means.

To compete just by signing better individuals is short term and offers no reliably consistent, competitive advantage.

To have your teams play a system, a team shape, that allows them to pass and move means you can slot a *superior individual* into a key position and he will thrive.

When he or they are not available, the system should allow the others to create chances and defend competently, regardless of the individual make-up of the team.

In the short term, the results may not improve, at least while the team adapts to the system and overcomes its own resistance to the changes. A team may half adopt the changes, not find instant success and partially return to the old ways.

The team may resist fully implementing the correct shape or will try to choose when it does so. This will lead to inconsistency in playing style and in the results gained from it.

It really is an all or nothing approach to the game. The manager and players must fully commit to implementing the system regardless of initial faults in it.

A system is a percentage thing.

The system is all about providing a structure and instructions for getting the ball into the opponent's last third as regularly as possible and, more importantly, with enough players to have full control of the ball, to set up a chance via the three ways to score in open play.

Having the ball in the attacking last third under control with enough attacking players to keep it there, will also lead to more corners, free kicks and penalties. The top teams' statistics show they receive more of these than the bottom teams.

Another problem with adopting *the correct shape in possession* as part of your system of play is that the opposition may respond in a like manner.

Many lower teams say they enjoy playing the *better* teams because they get to play a *better* standard of football, even though they may end up losing.

Losing, because the *better* team is more used to playing this system than they are.

If you are the better team, the defensive shape assumed by your opposition results as a direct consequence of your team's correct shape in possession.

You have stretched the pitch but not only for your team.

When the opposition regain possession, they are then often in the right shape to maintain it.

They are further inclined to do so after seeing your side keep its shape and play a pass-and- move game. They will however lack the practice in it.

I have outlined the correct shape as being fundamental for a pass-and-move style game.

It is still only a description of something that happens naturally whenever good football is played. The correct shape *is not seen enough* in local level football.

Expand with the ball, contract without.

Use the space on the pitch. Let the ball do the work.

It is just football common sense we have all heard before and if you can play with this common sense, you cannot help but have the right shape.

Football is a simple game.

It is a team game with the eleven cogs in the machine doing their part, in their area, to achieve an overall end. Eleven acting as one.

It gets complicated because convincing eleven different abilities, temperaments and personalities to play in a simple way, to achieve team goals, on a percentage basis is complicated.

However, you must convince each player of the need to fulfil his part in *a correct team shape* so that the team will profit from it over the period of the game or even games.

That is, in the long run.

Convince them that doing the right thing on the majority of occasions will bring the desired results in the end. The right thing is to play their part in the shape and *their part only*.

Players, in the main, should *stick to their task*, whether they are the full back, winger or centre half; and not get tempted into other areas of the pitch or into doing jobs better left to players in the other positions.

This helps the manager evaluate problems in the shape or playing staff.

If players are squeezing their own players; if both centre halves' are following forwards onto their full back's wing; if the full back plays beside his centre half at every opportunity or wingers are playing centrally it is very hard for a manager to put his finger on exactly what is going wrong or who is not performing.

If the central midfield is not performing and the winger goes inside to help, how can the manager see if it is the winger or the central midfielder failing in his job?

When **players stick to their allotted tasks**, any player who is failing to perform his task stands out for all to see. That player must improve his performance or be replaced.

With the right shape, you have two lines of players, two arched channels along which the ball can safely flow. With the shape to maintain possession achieved, you can now **use units of players to connect these two arched lines** and create an attacking move.

Shape is about your starting position. Movement gets you to the finishing position.

With the right shape you can begin to use pass-and-move as a strategy.

You can then begin to create the circumstances we need for scoring goals.

To score goals, we need to get in to the attacking last third of the pitch.

A team should have a main playing strategy that best uses the capabilities of its personnel, optimising its opportunities to get into the last third.

There are two normal ways to achieve this, with a combination of the two the best policy.

The long ball and *pass-and-move*. Both are only successful within the correct team shape.

Pass-and-move runs a chronological second to the *correct team shape* as the most important fundamental in improving lower league-level soccer, and is described in chapter 2.

2

Pass And Move

I maintain that the number one concept that you can try to get over to local league teams is **the correct team shape in possession**. This is a necessary starting point in order to be able to play a pass-and-move game of soccer.

Once your team sets up in the right shape, it is ready to distribute the ball safely via the players in the shape, to arrive in the attacking last third with the ball in good possession.

Remember the objects of the game in possession. The ultimate object is to score a goal. **There are three ways to score in open play**. They are all achieved in the attacking last third of the pitch. The primary object is, therefore, to get the ball into the attacking last third. See chapter 3, *Scoring a Goal*.

It is not enough just to get the *ball* into the attacking last third. You need players in there. The more players you can safely get into the last third in good possession of the ball, the greater your chances of creating one of the three ways to score.

Good possession means with the ball under control, facing the opponent's goal, with your head up and options for a pass.

The right shape first, combined with a pass-and-move game second, will enable your team to consistently arrive in the attacking last third and will therefore increase your team's chance of creating a goal-scoring opportunity.

With the right team shape in possession, the pass-and-move game first becomes possible.

This is because the angles and distances between teammates give them time and space to take a touch, get their head up, make a pass and move.

The increase in the size of the open angles and the physical distances between players makes it very difficult for teams with a local league fitness level to put pressure on the man in possession, before he has picked a pass to maintain possession.

With movement from the right shape, first-time passes can almost be played blind, in that players get to know the position of their teammate instinctively.

The ball can be knocked back or sideways into the space your teammate *should be in.* If he is consistently not there, we should fix the shape and movement first, not the passing.

Now we have the right starting shape, we need to hammer home the pass-and-move concept. The emphasis is always on **MOVE**. I should make the font bigger. It cannot be stressed enough, so I will repeat it, pass and **MOVE**.

Good movement often enables an easy pass. Bad movement or lack of movement requires pinpoint accuracy, timing and weight of pass.

Bad movement or lack of movement, in my opinion, is the biggest reason for turnover of ball possession in the local game.

Players are forced to take an opponent on, attempt a "wonder" pass or kick the ball aimlessly forward, when they have no teammates available.

If the movement is good, most players can get the passing right.

Local-level players tend to move only if they think they are going to get the ball. Local-level games look difficult and tight, as if there was no space on the park. Every pass keenly contested, easy passes a rarity.

With good movement by the players *who may not get the ball,* the standard of the game would change dramatically.

You often see a local team warming up before a match. Divided into two teams of five, six or seven, and using bibs, they play keep-ball. They prove remarkably good at it, considering they are doing it in a very confined area of the pitch.

A confidence-boosting familiarity with their own teammates as opposition and being uninhibited by having to go forward with the ball, they are free to **make runs and open angles** in all directions. They begin to talk, pass, shield the ball and move like the professionals.

When the game starts, it is a different story.

A typical simplified scenario in local soccer is this: a player has the ball in midfield; he has his head up and is looking for a pass.

The defenders behind him continue to mark their opponents and so are unavailable to receive a pass. They do not want the ball and do not encourage the midfielder to pass to them. In any case, the midfielder is already conditioned not to pass the ball back.

His wingers or forwards are marked and the thought in their heads is, "I am marked". The subliminal message being, "do not pass to me".

The thought in their heads should be, "I am marked; **I had better move, create space and try and get unmarked**".

The opposition sense that the midfielder has nobody to pass to and close him down, intent on a tackle. Wary of being caught in possession, the midfielder will not present himself sideways on shielding the ball, as might happen at a higher level.

This is because he knows he will not have the safe sideways or back pass available, even if he sets himself up to look for one. Therefore, the skill of shielding the ball in midfield is missing at local level, as it is rarely appropriate.

The midfielder under pressure has two options: take the man on or pass/kick the ball forward.

If one of his teammates does make a move, it will usually be a forward run, directly towards the end line. They will shout for the ball, demanding a perfectly timed pass delivered through the very narrow angle available, due to the steepness of their run.

The midfielder may decide to attempt this difficult pass, resulting in one of the following five outcomes.

1. The forward is caught offside, due to the steepness of his run and the necessary split- second timing of the pass not being in harmony.

2. An opposition defender will read the play, step into the narrow angle and cut off the pass.

3. The difficulty of the pass will prove too much and the ball will be wayward.

4. The midfielder misses his fleeting chance of delivering the ball and is caught in possession.

5. The midfielder will deliver a perfectly weighted, accurate and timely pass into the forward.

Now, anybody involved in local soccer knows which of these five outcomes is the most *unlikely*. It does not even have a 1 in 5 chance of success, more like 1 in 10.

It would appear that most local teams are happy with this 1 in 10 return, as they do not confront the problem, which is bad shape and bad movement.

Invariably, the player deemed at fault will be the midfielder, forced to attempt the pass. He is often moaned at by the forward for failing to deliver the wonder pass.

The man on the ball is King. Convincing your players of this will help cure bad movement. If your players can grasp and believe in this concept, their movement for each other will greatly improve.

They will genuinely want to help the man on the ball in order *to become* the man on the ball. In order to become the King.

They will not make hopeless runs, creating easily cut-out angles; or demand a pass timed exactly to their run and not timed to the passers' possibility to supply.

These players must think they are a bus. They have one predictable route and they dictate when they are leaving. The route suits them first and they do not wait for the passenger.

You see them running through an open angle into which a pass could be made, until there is no longer an angle for the pass available. It is as though they are saying, "I'm off, I'm on a schedule, I can't stop, and I'm the 46A".

These players obviously believe they are already the King, even though they do not yet have the ball. They need to **learn how to get the ball**.

If they really believed this concept, they would do all they could to please. Making impossible runs, then moaning at the King would be anathema.

What they should do to help the King and maybe eventually become King is this. They should **make it easy for the man on the ball to pass the ball**.

They should make runs which increase their chance of actually receiving the ball, timing the run to match the present King's schedule, not their own.

They should serve the King, not the other way around.

Many times you see a player set off, demanding an instant through-ball when the midfielder is still fighting for possession, with his head down, the ball bouncing, not under control.

This bus waits for no man and has already left.

It is vitally important that **the run be timed to suit the timescale of the man in possession**. This is a basic to all good footballers.

They watch the body shape of the King and make their move suddenly and decisively, just as they read that he is in a position to supply.

Not before he is ready and not too late.

The principal of timing your run or opening an angle to match the man in possession's needs and capabilities is fundamental to the pass-and-move game.

It is a requirement for players in all positions.

It is part of reading the game, part of being a good player.

Life is about timing, and **the pass-and-move game of soccer is all about timing**: the timing and synchronicity of the movements and the pass.

Too often, players hold onto the ball just because they can. They delay passing, taking unnecessary touches. This has a disruptive effect on the movement of a team, clogging it up as the ball struggles to flow through the shape.

As soon as you see a pass that will **keep the ball moving through the shape**, stop yourself from being contained or put the ball into safer or better possession; you must make that pass.

Whether you are under pressure to do so or not and whether you yet see a clear attacking purpose to the move, continue to keep the ball moving.

Crisp accurate passing, to feet. This avoids the hospital ball and gives the opposition no chance to intervene, whilst saving you time and wasting theirs' in useless pursuit.

Passing is good for passing's sake. The quicker the better. Whilst the ball is being successfully passed, the opposition is always caught short of where it wants to be.

Eventually, one or more of them may fail to even try to close down the ball or its recipients; and that is when the killer forward pass that opens them up becomes an easy pass.

The ball never gets tired, which is why you let the ball do the work. Like the matador tiring the bull by getting it to attack something that is never there, your opposition will tire.

Quick passing encourages sharp movement, as the supporting players cannot hang about in providing their movement.

The ball begins to tick over, creating a rhythm, which at best puts the opposition to sleep. They are caught between closing down one player or the other as the ball is moving faster than they can react.

The momentum of a move seems to grow with each quick pass, as if with each pass a fraction of time is saved. The opposition, as if completing a beep test, eventually cannot plug the gap and the killer pass presents itself.

A quick pass-and-move tempo keeps your team sharp and concentrating. You cannot but concentrate if you are doing things fast. **Slow tempo encourages slow thought** and leads to concentration lapses.

Triangles of players appear and disappear all over the pitch in support of the man on the ball. Those players within the King's passing range, say 5-40 yards, create an angle or make runs that move the opposition to suit him. The other players maintain the team shape to receive the ball later in the move.

These fluid triangles around the man on the ball are similar wherever on the pitch they occur. Their purpose is to maintain and progress possession.

If the man in possession decides it is too risky to progress this move by continuing going forward, there should be a safe pass available.

This position is directly or diagonally behind him 10-25 yards. This position is usually safe because the opposition prioritise covering the forward movements.

Two other teammates, also 10 to 25 yards from him, provide an option within the man on the ball's eye-line. One may be a more speculative movement and one a little easier for the man on the ball. One going long, one coming short.

The important thing is that these two players providing the forward pass or the pass that will progress the move are *never static*. **If they are static they will be marked**, the pass may be read and the ball lost.

If they provide an option which is not taken or which is immediately covered by their marker, they must move again and quickly provide a new option.

They pop into view, offer themselves fleetingly and if not taken up on the offer, move again, **creating space for somebody else** or becoming **the third man running**.

The triangle is not in a consistent position or shape, but its angles and distances constantly adjust to suit the man on the ball and to lose markers.

When the ball is switched away from the supporting triangle and away from that area, that triangle breaks up and its members resume the team shape.

A new triangle, edging further up the pitch, forms around the new King and similar movement to progress or maintain the ball begins again.

In this way, the ball can be kept in safe possession until the team arrives deep into the attacking last third, where it is time to prepare an attack on goal

In match reality, **the triangles around the man on the ball can get tight**, especially around the touchlines and in the last third. The opposition, if they press well, have the ability to squeeze in close if a pass or the control is less than perfect.

The unit in possession must support the man closer if he is under extreme pressure, with his head down protecting the ball. They need to get in his line of vision and for this they get nearer to him than they would normally prefer in open play.

The movement to open angles is now more intricate, **shielding the ball** becomes **a necessary skill**, the footwork quickens and the passing becomes more one-touch.

They have to **think as a unit. The unit has the ball, not the individual** in that unit. If possession of the ball is lost or maintained, it is lost or maintained by the unit.

The rest of the team keeps its shape, awaiting the outcome. The object of the unit in control is to retrieve this potential ball-loss situation, and play the ball out of this tight area into a space that you are in better control of.

In this way, the tight squeeze of your opponents works against them if you successfully manage to switch play and can advance finding them light elsewhere on the pitch.

Good movement will mean that defence and midfield players consistently have up to **three choices of pass** available: a **safe** backward or square pass, a **maintenance** square or forward pass and the attacking (often speculative) **forward** pass.

Maintenance in this case means maintaining the progress of a particular move, whereas the safe pass may be the prelude to a new build-up move.

When you can pass forward, you should. When you cannot pass forward you pass sideway's and when you cannot pass sideway's you pass backward. You must **keep the pressure on the opposition** without negligently losing possession.

Decisions, decisions. In football as in life, **the key to your success**.

The footballing shape of two curved lines in possession is designed to facilitate the passing game. The curved lines distort subtly as players pop out of the curved line to support and create the triangle effect around the man in ball possession.

The curved line allows the ball to be switched from one side of the pitch to the other without majorly confronting the opponents.

It is in the curved back line where you outnumber the opposition that so often the momentum of a pass-and-move game begins.

Let us **start a** theoretical **pass-and-move game in the back line**, based necessarily on the typical team shape and movement of professional teams.

If, as a lower league-level team, we can see and understand this playing style in our minds, then we may be able to replicate *parts of it* at the weekend.

The right full back has the ball. He is close to the throw line, just entering the middle third of the pitch. If he looks over his left shoulder, he should find one of his centre halves 25 or so yards diagonally behind him.

This centre half is offering him a safe out if the right back cannot play the ball reliably forwards or if he just wants to switch the side of play.

A centre midfielder should be offering himself 15-25 yards away diagonally left in front of the right back, the mirror image of the centre half offering the safe out.

The right winger 20 or so yards ahead of the right back should be moving from the touchline to 20 yards in field and back again, **constantly looking to spin his marker and open an angle** in which he can receive the ball.

When he temporarily moves inside, he may create space on the wing for his full back or forward to exploit, if the chance comes.

The target man centre forward should be offering himself by coming towards the full back maybe from 40 to 25 yards away.

The other centre forward may be offering to chase a longer diagonal pass over the target man or making a cross-run into the space vacated by him.

He may be pushing along their back line, probing the gaps between the opposition centre halves and fullbacks. **He keeps the top of the pitch stretched**.

See the position chapters for information on specific individual movement.

All other players for the team in possession, *through subtle movement*, should be maintaining their positions and therefore their shape, ready to become involved should the ball come into their areas. They are set up and ready for ball loss or ball possession.

What we see here is a disciplined team with a good shape offering good movement. The right back has a safe pass behind him created by the centre half, which also conforms to the maxim of not leaving the last man on the ball.

This pass from full back to centre half is probably the *most common* in professional soccer and the *least common* in the local game.

If the right back chooses to do this, the centre half can quickly play the ball another 25 yards or so left, to his partner centre half. From here, the ball can be moved on up to the left back and from there into the midfield or strikers and back as the move progresses.

The opposition, with normally only two forward players available to close the ball down in these areas, will find it difficult to do so. If the centre halves are closed down, they will have the goalkeeper as their safe out-pass.

If the goalie has the ball comfortably at his feet, **we have a perfect opportunity to begin pass-and-move** again, this time from as far back as it gets.

This is now the same scenario as the goal-kick situation mentioned previously in the team shape chapter. The centre halves quickly part to each corner edge of the 18-yard box. The full backs push 30 yards up from the goal line and wide.

The forwards, wingers and attacking midfielder attempt through good movement to push the opposition back as far as they will go. **This all happens as soon as the goalie gets on the ball**. He might kick it long so the opposition have to cover our forward movement.

The opponents, with only two or at most three players, should find themselves with too much space to cover around our keeper to win the ball here. If the centre halves are covered, the **holding midfielder should come short in the middle** to offer the safe pass to the keeper.

Now we have two full backs, two centre halves, a central midfielder and the goalie starting a possession game where they seriously outnumber the opposition.

This is a **fundamental at professional level** and if you have a goalie who can pass the ball under minimal pressure, then it is possible at our level.

If your goalie cannot do that and you want to play pass-and-move, which begins best from the back, then you will have to get a new keeper.

You are attracting just two or three opposition players high to press you whilst your forward players push their teammates back. This creates the space in between to start *good* possession.

The full backs, by going wide and high, may squeeze their winger from the wing into midfield. This is often intentional in the first phase of build-up play from the back.

The winger requires now to be picked up in forward central midfield, allowing the attacking midfielder to drop a little, also still requiring a marker.

This all gives the holding midfielder a chance to play in the space created around your own defensive last third.

Here, with good movement, **opening his body side-on to the play**, careful not to create steep angles to receive the ball, he pops the ball between full backs and centre halves, evading any pressers.

If he can turn and play it forward, he will. **He should be half turned** already.

The opponents have to mark from nearest their goal first. This pushing action by your forward players, claiming space in their half, stretching them wide, and keeping them busy means they cannot *also press* high up the pitch.

If the opponent's defence is naive enough to enforce a high line, up to the halfway line, then it should be a simple task for one of your back line or the keeper to place an angled ball over the top of them.

In this case, you have created a goal threat simply by setting up ready to play from the back.

If the opponents do successfully press the ball, then the goalie or a defender simply clears it up field. Nothing lost. In the professional game, the opposition usually drops back and concedes this first phase possession.

By this means of simply moving the ball back and forth along the defensive line, using the holding midfielder as a link, a professional team will edge up to the centre of the pitch, maintaining good possession.

Why this does not happen at local level is to do with **belief and concentration**.

The players do not believe the team members are good enough to each play their sometimes subtle but crucial parts in starting a game from the very back.

They are also not prepared to **focus enough mental energy on the game** and its component parts, preferring to let the game pass by like a student kick-around in the park, saving their thought processes and self-discipline for the working week. See chapter 18, *The Manager*.

In fact, if you **collectively use your soccer brain**, the game becomes easier and your individual technical faults become less obvious. You can gain space to play through your good thinking rather than your good touch. You can **play better than you individually are**.

When some just stand and watch, pass-and-move will fall apart. You must all commit to it.

Whether you do or you don't, the theory will remain true.

Use the defensive line to start and maintain possession and to safely switch sides with the ball. Only certain players make themselves available at each point in this possession.

The rest maintain discipline, awaiting the moment that the ball can come to their area before employing movement designed to help the man on the ball continue the move.

Whenever a player is in possession, at least two to five teammates should be moving or taking up a position to help him maintain possession and continue the move.

One of these teammates may offer the "over the shoulder" safe back pass, one a not-so-safe forward or square pass, and one a speculative creative pass seeking to open up the opposition.

All these players are properly supporting the player on the ball in different ways.

They have **formed triangles** around him, making it difficult for the opposition to close him and them down at the same time.

If you have triangles of support you will become more confident on the ball and will get your head up and play, safe in the knowledge that you have an out-pass when under pressure.

Should the ball be lost in this position, **the support triangle becomes the first defence. One player pressurises** and tries to instantly win the ball back or force the move away from a vulnerable area.

One squeezes in support, in case the first defender gets beaten, and to further restrict the angle of attack available to the opponent in possession.

Another acts as cover, reading a medium-length ball out from this position to an opponent, hitting a space, created or vacated, by your players squeezing the ball.

The rest **squeeze onto their men** and create a solid defensive barrier.

In possession, the teammates that have not supported him but have maintained their positions, are offering a switch via a long ball into their areas.

If the opposition have pressed to squeeze the man in possession and his support triangle, then he can switch the ball out into an area not filling up with the opposition.

If they are squeezing the ball in numbers, then they must be short elsewhere, and the speculative **switch ball into space** can lead to a one-on-one contest for the ball.

This contest is often what a forward or winger thrives on and is particularly suited to the local-level game.

The **support movement is varied** in its angles and directions. It is not all running away from the man on the ball in a direct line into the opposition's half and towards the goal.

The pass chosen can guarantee that ball possession is maintained or it can be a more risky forward pass to move play towards the opponent's last third, where goal-scoring chances are created.

Safe passes to maintain possession would normally take precedence over speculative passing. The speculative pass can always come later in the move.

Professional teams can be so patient in this regard that they can go from being in the attacking last third to being back at their own keeper, rather than concede possession.

Possession-maintenance passes have a soporific effect on the opposition. Professional teams, especially Barcelona, can mesmerise opposition players by the countless amount of maintenance passes.

Until suddenly one of the opposition has dropped his concentration, gone asleep in soccer parlance, and a killer pass can be safely played to bring the team into goal creation areas, i.e. into the attacking last third.

For professional teams, **possession-maintenance passes create a rhythm** and give a momentum to the game. They can dictate the pace of the game, slowing it down and speeding it up. They choose when to risk possession and when to play safe.

Keeping the ball with pass-and-move tires the opposition, mentally and physically. Tired opponents make mistakes and give away fouls.

The rhythm of good soccer is the rhythm of life. **Slow slow quick quick slow**. Slow and secure in the early build up, quick and decisive in the killer forward thrust, ending with a cool calm finish.

In local league, there is very little possession-maintenance passing. The dominant pass is the steep forward attacking/speculative pass. We force the play nonstop.

Possession-maintenance passes can get you far up the pitch without risking turning the ball over. Barcelona would be so good at the short easy passes and the quick expert movement that enables them; they can seemingly arrive in numbers around the opponent's box simply by always picking the easiest obvious pass.

By this means of playing the ball, say, 20 yards forward, then 10 yards back and safely square within the lines of four until a *killer pass* emerges, there is a gradual edging up into the last third without greatly risking possession.

I am not advocating that local teams try to emulate Barcelona. Players at that level have a supreme fitness, touch and vision, allowing runs, and creating movement that are two and three passes ahead of the move, let alone supporting the man on the ball.

I am saying that at local-league level, even one or two maintenance passes may move the opposition around enough. Enough to enable a player to get the ball under control, his head up, and with time to play it safely into the last third to a teammate.

In soccer, time and space are the same thing.

Movement creates space, which provides time to play.

Ball-watching is not only **the enemy of good defending**, it is **also the enemy of good movement**. Players who ball-watch tend to be spectators, rooted to the spot, and do not create quick, open angles. If they do move, they will be blinkered, predictable, one-dimensional runs that the opposition will cover.

If they are lucky enough to get the ball, they will not know where they or anybody else is and will either spend *move destroying* time on the ball, getting their bearings, or make a rash and uninformed decision.

You have to glance around you all the time to get the full picture, to be fully informed and to be able to react correctly.

You must **constantly check your position**, that of your colleagues and the opponents. You should be considering your options for constructive movement, either showing for the man on the ball or creating space for a teammate's benefit. You cannot switch off.

Look around, take your eyes off the ball for a second, wherever you might be on the pitch. Then you will know where to move in order to help and where you are if you get the ball.

I know that is easier said than done. The whole book is easier said than done. It is back to *focus or concentration*. How good are you prepared to be?

If, as an individual, you have the ball and you play with blinkers on instead of wing mirrors, you are denying yourself many passing opportunities and will find the game tight and lacking options.

The movement and pass is not always in front of you.

You do not have to go down the cul-de-sac proposed for you by the opponents.

You do not have to make an elaborate Cruyff turn to be able to check and look elsewhere for an easier route of progress.

Yet it helps if you can, and all **players**, whatever the level, **should have a change of direction in their skill set**. More importantly, they should learn when to use it.

At local level, the object is to get the ball safely out of the first curved line of the defence and into the second curved line of midfield and wingers.

If this is done as the theory suggests, the team should still be in its attacking shape and a new triangle of support should spring up around the new man in possession.

Now, with the ball in the midfield attacking arched shape, the opposition have the numbers to put the wingers and midfielders under pressure. It is important that the defence and centre forwards provide an outlet backward or forward pass for the midfield players.

The full backs can do this by keeping their width and distance from the midfielder to become his *over-the-shoulder* safe pass. See chapter 9, *Fullbacks*.

The centre halves do this by losing their forward marker and providing a safe 20-yard or so back pass in the event that the midfielder gets turned or pressured into doing so. See chapter 8, *Centre Halves*.

The forwards do this by presenting toward the midfielder with a well-timed short run off the centre back or threatening a run in behind. See chapter 6, *Strikers*.

Players who make themselves available should be the *maximum distance* from the man on the ball. **The maximum distance that does not risk interception of the pass.**

This makes it harder for the opposition to press, stretches the pitch, and the ball can gain territory faster. Sometimes, of course, the maximum distance will prove quite near and play does tend to get closed down on the pitch extremities.

In the midfield-arched shape, triangles of support for the man on the ball appear and disappear. The **diamond of the holding and attacking midfielder** becomes apparent, facilitating a constant central midfield triangle of support in possession, opening up both wings as possible avenues of penetration.

Not everyone who moves to make a pass angle can receive the ball, but the fact that more than one movement is made and more than one angle is open, means that the likelihood of a successful pass is increased. **One player's move creates space for another**.

The likelihood of the opposition not adequately tracking a move is increased, and space for a breakthrough pass can suddenly emerge where none was foreseen.

The movement approaching the opponent's last third needs to be sharper than that which might suffice in the defensive back-line. There are more opponents and there is greater necessity for these opponents to recover the ball.

It is about running into the channels between and behind the defence, *followed instantly by the ball*. At any decent level, you need to work on your movement to achieve this.

Players need to make clever runs in behind and across defenders, changing direction in quick spurts. They do not even need to have a finished move in their heads when they are doing this. In fact, if they wait until they have seen the required move, the defence will probably have seen it too. **Movement is good for movement's sake**.

You may run all game trying to open angles and create space. Most of your movement will be checked by the opposition or be unseen by the man on the ball and left unrewarded.

If you get any payback at all from your movement in the entire match, it might still be enough to create a goal and win the game. The trouble is you do not know which of your runs will prove the successful one. You have to make all of them to find out.

The lower local-league mentality of only moving when you have a good chance of receiving the ball is wrong and needs to be ditched if there is going to be improvement and if pass-and-move is to realistically become a lower-level strategy.

The opposition may move out of a good position to counter a run that they would have better left unchecked. **Movement causes the opposition to move** and can create a space that was not previously there.

For example, a striker wants to receive a ball from a full back or midfielder in a specific place, say played into a channel towards the corner of the 18-yard box. He should not stand waiting in that space. He should not move too early into that space.

The winger may help create the space by moving towards his own full back or midfielders offering a short maintenance pass. This may take the opposition full back away from the space the centre forward is looking to attack.

The forward will make initial movement toward the centre of the goal, trying to push the centre half back and into the middle, trying to start the run on his blindside.

When he is sure the space is available, i.e. the opposition full back has followed his winger out of his area and his teammate is ready to pass, he can make his quick move into the space towards the wing.

The winger can then turn and make a centre forward's run and provide a target for a possible cross from the striker now winger.

Another run or move not common enough to the local game is the square/across run as opposed to the very common forward/steep run.

This is a very productive move in seemingly tight situations and one the opposition central defence hesitates to track, as it may bring him out of his desired position and create a space where he previously was.

Yet, if he doesn't track it, an accurate pass could see the forward bend his run onto the ball.

This square run across a central defensive pair by a forward can produce or widen a gap and allow a midfielder to make a late steep run into the space created.

When you start your run, you do not have to see a space to run into. It may seem that you are leaving one marked area to make a run into another. Your **movement creates** the space. You drag a marker slightly out of position and that may open a space for a teammate.

In another example, a forward, winger or midfielder wants to receive a pass played up to him from behind. However, he is tightly marked and would prefer to receive the ball in this same position but turned and facing his marker.

He first makes a move at half pace, say 10 yards to the left of where he may eventually want the ball, followed by his marker.

Meanwhile, a ball-maintenance move is going on behind him, as his teammates see no obvious credible forward pass and prefer to wait for the right moment.

He then makes a short quicker *forward run*, as if he wants the ball played steep, again hopefully tracked by his marker.

Within a few yards and with his marker turned and running towards his own goal, the player changes direction and sprints the diagonal back toward the space he had initially foreseen as creatable.

His teammates, who have been playing maintenance passes, awaiting just such timed creation, now release the ball to him. Having made a few yards space, he can now receive it, open bodied and facing his opponent. You **go long to get the ball short**.

They have successfully moved the ball forward and are in good safe possession where they can set triangles up again to protect it and progress the move using a similar procedure.

There are specific movement descriptions in all the *position* chapters.

Good movement means movement by several players, not just by the obvious recipient of the most likely pass. **Movement can move the opposition** out of their preferred starting point and confuse them in their choice of which movement to confront as a priority.

Good movement is normally not just a one-piece forward movement, as seen in countless local-league matches up and down the land.

It usually consists of one move to take an opponent away from the desired space, one move to get some momentum in the wrong direction, and then the third decisive run into the space now created.

If that **third decisive run** is made **by a different player**, even better.

This is all timed to match the man on the ball's readiness to pass. The first two parts of the movement may go on regularly without the chance to put the third conclusive part into action. However, other opportunities may arrive to the man on the ball, partly because of this movement going on in front of him.

Cutting across players and running square opens the angle up and makes a pass easier for the man on the ball. Steep forward runs create narrow angles and demand passes that are more accurate.

Diagonal runs, steep ball; steep runs, diagonal ball is a mantra of good soccer.

One touch, give-and-go passes with good movement can leave an opponent stranded.

Good movement creates space quickly, in between and behind the opposition. A move towards the ball, covered by a marker, creates space behind you for another player to run into. This is true all over the pitch.

Good movement consists of feints, dummy runs and crossovers, where players quickly swap positions. It presupposes an alert soccer mind and a willingness to work the opposition's and your own legs, before making the actual ball-receiving run.

Sometimes, standing still constitutes good movement.

If you are already in a good position and unmarked and there is enough alternative movement going on to keep the opposition busy, then your decisive move is already complete. Standing still can be your invisibility cloak.

Alas, at local-league level, you are as likely to see a player leaving a perfectly good position and an open angle, making himself suddenly unavailable to the man on the ball.

Again, this is an example of the bus driver syndrome, with the player working to his own prescribed timetable and route.

The choreography of the pass-and-move game is to a degree instinctive and off-the-cuff, but it is also a team skill that can be practised. Without good and timely movement, accurate and timely passes will not be possible.

The movement within professional teams and by good players is markedly superior to that seen at local-league level. They are better, fitter players with more time to prepare.

The angles and runs may be slicker, quicker and more plentiful but in theory, at lower level, we should still be doing a relative version of them.

The lack of patience, concentration, belief and therefore confidence prevents it.

Without good movement, the chances of getting good possession in the opponent's last third are greatly diminished. That, in turn, diminishes the chances of creating the three ways to score in open play.

One reason for bad or no movement in local soccer is that once a player is marked, he often resigns himself to that fact. He decides he can only get the ball in *this position* and the defender has *this position* taken.

Even if he makes a little run, his marker will cover it and he won't get the ball because he is moving away from its predictable path; so what would be the point?

The point is, of course, that movement is good for movement's sake. **Movement creates space. Space means time to play**. The effect of a run toward or move away may not be apparent in advance but it can create fleeting but fatal gaps in the opposition's ranks.

The player providing the movement may not receive the ball in the initial stage of the move but by creating space for a teammate, he may become the ultimate beneficiary of his own creation. He may become **the third man in the move**.

This is how it can be presented to less *team aware* players to encourage them to move when the chance of them personally receiving the ball look slim.

Good players run, off the ball, for the team constantly.

All the movement of a good team around the ball confuses the opposition; they are not sure which move will attract the ball.

A defender (*everybody* in the team without possession) can delay deciding which of two moves to counter and end up countering neither. Two of them may counter the same move, leaving another attacker (*everybody* in the team with possession) free to receive a pass.

Movement is crucial and like team shape, a successful passing game is dependent upon it. With the right shape and well-timed clever movement, the passing game of soccer in possession becomes a pleasure to take part in and watch.

Good movement delivers more forays into the opponent's defensive third, where the ball is in good possession, i.e. head up, facing the opponent, with sufficient teammates available and therefore more chances to create goal-scoring opportunities.

In reality in local league, if you get the ball into the midfield-arched line in the opposition half, head up and under control, the next pass or move can be speculative.

With the ball in your possession in the attacking last third, one of the three ways to score may be promptly pursued. This is to avoid the risk of missing the opportunity to do so, by striving for an even better start point.

Looking for a perfect safe route to goal is one for the professionals.

Local league can afford to be more direct once in the opponent's half and especially last third. We do not want to attempt ball maintenance beyond our capabilities or indeed if it is not necessary to do so.

Overplaying of the ball in the attacking last third without advanced level movement is often a local-level problem. Direct play, indeed **simply putting it in the box, from the last third can be enough to create chances**.

I am not advocating too many passes or demanding too much in terms of movement and mental alertness by local players with other, more important things, on their minds.

However, the theory of pass-and-move is a good one and has been proven at the highest level. The intention for local clubs should be to put a relative amount of thought and method into ball possession and chance creation, employing pass-and-move as a major strategy.

If we do not make *any* maintenance passes, good movement will not present, as good movement often requires time and cooperation to set up.

It also needs to be set up away from the prying eyes of defenders. This will not be possible if you are always the obvious intended recipient of the predictable pass.

The key word in pass-and-move is **MOVE**. The key to good movement is timing. **The timing of the movement matched to the man on the ball's possibility to supply**.

Communication plays an important role in soccer and no more so than in a successful pass-and-move game.

In a professional team, the communication can be very subtle as only the necessary is vocalised: constant yet discerning *advice, warnings and commands*.

In the lower levels, background noise of ill-advised demands for the ball and conflicting or panicky instructions to the man in possession can fill the air and confuse.

Genuinely beneficial advice is either not given or goes unheeded in this jumble of sound.

The marshalling and controlling of the team's defences and direction of play should be the vocal remit of just one or two experienced players, one of whom should be the captain.

This constant conducting of team shape and tempo demands a unified voice.

Calls for the ball should be timed to match the possibility to deliver, and avoided if that possibility is remote.

However, we are each other's eyes and ears on the pitch and that means **nobody has the right to remain silent**. Each unit of *players must communicate well* to be a successful unit.

We do not have eyes in the back of our heads and sometimes our view is impeded; or the angles and distances involved do not allow you to make a decision unaided.

If a player has his head down, eye on the ball, is under pressure or running at speed, it is hard for him to know exactly what is happening around him.

By the time he gets the ball under control and looks up, the situation may have changed. Communication keeps him informed.

Advice is given as a pre-warning or to provide an option the player on the ball may wish to consider. It can set the scene for him from an additional perspective, calming him down, reassuring him, and encouraging informed decision-making.

Warnings are given if the player is in imminent danger of being dispossessed or if an opponent is sneaking blindside or needs to be marked. They alert players to threats.

Commands are issued when the carrying out of the desired action only has a fleeting opportunity to succeed or if that instruction is without doubt the most acceptable course to pursue. In which case, it should be pursued as quickly as possible. Hence, a command is required to ensure speedy compliance instead of dalliance.

Warnings and commands may sound heated or confrontational to the inexperienced ear. Only bad or inexperienced players take them personally.

Advice should always be delivered calmly. All are necessary if possession is to be maintained, but only as necessary as they are useful.

Useless sound is a distraction, an irritant and a hindrance to pass-and-move.

A team that communicates well has a radar, a traffic-control system that is a real aid in maintaining possession and progressing up the pitch.

The various verbal utterances used in a game should be intelligible, relevant, consistent and concise.

There is presumably a glossary somewhere of soccer terms and commands, which differ only in translation, not in meaning, throughout the world of soccer.

In many situations you will need to **tag on some verbal information when delivering your pass** or playing your supporting role in a unit's movement.

The most common and necessary, if *pass and move* is to be successful, are those that advise the player of something he may not be able to see, whilst receiving or carrying the ball.

For example: — "Turn on it!" — "Time!" — "Head up!" — "Trap it!" — "Hold it!" — "Man on!" or "House!" — "Away!" — "Look right!" — "Look left!" — "Check!" or "Stop and turn!"…

These are all short, simple and standardised. A good player will both say them and react positively upon hearing them.

Just don't say them all at once…

They give your teammate information that he needs if he is to be able to concentrate on the ball whilst under pressure from the opposition.

They save him time looking around, make him aware of his options and help him make the right decision for the team.

Get your shape right first. Then, from these staged starting postures, it will be possible, *yes, at lower local-league level*, to apply pass-and-move throughout the various positions.

Safely and effectively moving the ball up the pitch and into the opponent's danger area where, also in a calculated fashion, you can proceed to attack the goal.

If you do not believe this, you will not be able to do this.

The alternative to the pass-and-move game is often touted as the long-ball game. In reality, the *long ball* and *pass-and-move* are parts of the same game. Some teams use it more, as a match to their personnel, but they still use it within the pass-and-move game.

In the pass-and-move game, the long ball would be considered a big switch or a ball into good space and is probably better described as a long, albeit hopeful, pass.

It deserves a separate chapter and this comes after the third chronologically inevitable fundamental (if you get the first two right), scoring a goal.

3

Scoring A Goal

A crucial and satisfying part of soccer is scoring a goal. Goals are relatively rare and hard to come by, with 0-0 being a common enough result that is almost unique to this sport.

You will not win many games if you only score one goal. You will not win many games if you concede more than one.

Most people prefer a game where the winner is the team trying to score more rather than the team trying to concede the least. However, it is hard to be up one end scoring goals when the opposition is down your end trying to do likewise.

Therefore, a sound defence that takes the ball away from the opposing team is the start to goal scoring and a necessity if you wish to score more than the opposition.

Defending, like goal scoring, is an individual and a team skill and is covered in the "position" chapters.

Three ways to score

There are only three ways to score from open play. Halfway-line goals á la Beckham or Alonso, and goalkeepers' wind-assisted punts are exceptions that prove the rule. More importantly, the three ways all happen in the last third of the pitch.

1. Cross

A cross from the wings with the forwards or midfielders' attacking the ball as it arrives into the penalty area.

2. Shot

A direct shot from anywhere within the last third.

3. One-on-one

A one-on-one, against the goalkeeper. This can be created deliberately through a good pass, a successful dribble through the defence, or fortunately through a defensive mistake by the opposition.

The object is therefore to get into the opposition's defensive last third in order to attempt any of the three ways to score.

The right team shape and movement, with long and short passing, combine to get a few players quickly or, with patience, more players into the attacking last third.

The more attacking players in the attacking last third, the more opportunities to create goal chances. In counter attack, with attackers moving the ball rapidly forward, it is the least number of defensive players in the attacking last third that will lead to a good chance.

However a team manages it, once in the opponent's last third the players should now switch on to what they have to do. They should either quickly, in a counter-attack situation, or patiently embark on one of the three ways to score.

At lower local level, we may promptly pursue the first chance that presents. Waiting for a better chance may require more intricate ball passing and movement. That could lead to ball loss before a clearer chance is revealed. These are moments in the game that will test your players' decision-making skills.

There are three choices or avenues they are looking at to provide a goal chance.

Cross

Most goals come from crosses. The most dangerous of crosses come from the wing, behind the defence and near to the goal line. **Low crosses produce the most goals**.

Crosses that come from *near the goal line* give the attackers the best chance of scoring, as the attacker's momentum is towards the goal and they are close to the goal.

These crosses also find defenders, with their momentum towards goal and close to the goal, and are thus hardest to defend.

With playing offside no longer an option, the defenders have a real emergency on their hands.

A cross can come from the wing area in any part of the attacking last third and many teams will cross the first chance they get.

This is the right policy if you have good attackers of the ball in the box, are running out of time or if you fear losing the opportunity to cross, trying to get a player nearer the goal line.

In fact, at lower local level, it is **rarely a bad policy to put the ball in the box** from any position in the last third. It encourages your midfield and attackers into the box and even the most relaxed and cool defenders can begin to panic, as the ball gets closer to the goal.

Things happen when the ball goes into the 18-yard box. A lot of the hard work has been done if you have arrived in the opponent's last third in good ball possession, so why not cash in what you already have won, i.e. a cross into the box.

Crosses can cause havoc in a defence that might otherwise appear impregnable when attacked head on, through the centre.

Defensive blunders, goalkeeping errors, bizarre own goals and cross-cum-shot goals all make crosses into the box from the last third the most productive of goal scoring plays.

The cross must come first. Encourage your players to cross the ball whenever they find themselves on the wing in the last third and in a position to do so.

When your forwards and midfielders realise that their team crosses the ball into the box, often and early, they will make anticipatory runs into the 18-yard box.

The more goals they score from these crosses, the more confidence they will have in making the runs and the quality of the runs and movement in the box will improve.

The attackers must **make a variety of runs** so that the cross does not beat all of them. They should make a near post and a far post run. The other winger should be trying to come in late at the far post. They should have a different depth to their runs. This is to ensure the cross does not go in front or behind all of them at the same time.

They can change their runs and bend their runs. They should **make team runs** where someone might drag a defender away, e.g. to the near post as the cross goes far.

When a cross is coming into the box you must **attack the ball as a team**, not as individuals. When one of you scores, the team scores. Diversionary movement that disrupts the defence provides the space and time needed for a teammate to make a successful finish.

The point is that the runs should be varied, decisive and creative. **A good run can turn a bad cross into a good one**, just as we get decent crosses wasted by bad movement.

I often see a cross failing to beat the first man and the cross is criticised as a bad one. The team has four players waiting for the ball long and not one of them thought of running in front of the defensive first man, just in case the cross was short.

If one of them does and manages to flick the ball on, suddenly we hear it was a good cross.

If a cross is coming from the right wing, you might enter the box tracked by your opponent. You can speed up and bend your run left, threatening to pass behind your marker's back and heading for the far post.

When you get him turned slightly to cover this move you can quickly cut across him, head for the near post and be first to the cross.

This **getting across your defender in the box** leads to many goals. It can happen without any dummy run, if your marker is ball-watching or has set himself up at a bad angle to you. He will not see your blindside move until it is too late to react to it.

In local league, it is not always possible to practice attacking runs for various reasons. For me, **it is a state of mind** anyway. If their mind is focussed, they will make a decent run.

So encourage your forward players to get into the box, some early, some late and to **vary their runs** in an attempt to make the best of all types of crosses. The wingers must try to **make late runs**, blindside of the opposition, arriving at the far post.

You have the cross and the movement...the next step is the finish.

Finishing half and quarter chances is an art in itself. But here is some brief, **percentage-based finishing** advice for the easier crossed chance that may help a striker concentrate in the box.

Flick the ball on and into danger areas or teammates if you cannot get a decent goal-ward strike. Keep the chance alive. There is no point in *defending* the ball safely back to the keeper or putting it out tamely for a goal kick.

Make runs expecting the ball to come to you. Visualise it coming to you and scoring. Be prepared to meet it technically well and strike it goal-wards. **Expect to score**.

As you make your run into the box, take your eye off the ball crosser for a brief moment or two. Look at the goal; look at the position of the defenders and the goalkeeper before returning your attention to the crosser.

Now, when the cross comes in and you are fortunate enough that your run was the chosen one, you will have a natural photo image in your head of where everything relevant is.

This is a much harder thing to do than it sounds, but with an image in your mind of the position of the opposition and of the goal, your finishing can improve massively.

You may realise that you can take a touch or that you must strike first time, and to which area you should strike it. The extra information can do wonders for your confidence.

This kind of photo imaging of your position requires immense powers of concentration; or as the Americans might say, focus. You will be rewarded for it.

When the blood is pumping and in the heat of the moment, it takes a cool head to take your eye off the ball and look around you moments before a cross comes in.

Jump early to win your header if needs be. Jumping early can take a defender's air space.

Most importantly, **get the ball on target**. If the ball's arrival is awkward or bumpy, rather than blast it, choose to pass or trap it into the net. See also the chapter on attacking corners.

Shot

If you don't shoot, you won't score. We say it is a simple game and nothing exemplifies that so much as letting fly from 30 yards. All tactics and defensive systems can go out the window when a ball is hit hard into the top corner.

Realistically, shooting anywhere around the 18-yard box to 25 yards out is to be positively encouraged. If you have more shots on target than the opposition, you are guaranteed to win. *Statistically guaranteed*, that is.

Using pass-and-move to get your midfield players into the last third will significantly improve your chances to shoot from these distances.

Pass-and-move will mean that you should be able to get as many as six or seven players into the attacking last third with the ball in good possession.

Good possession means with the ball under control, facing the opponent's goal, with your head up and options of a pass.

Your first inclination may be to try to get down the wings and attempt a cross.

You may attempt a through ball to get a teammate one-on-one with the goalkeeper.

Either of these can lead to a shot from 18-25 yards out. When you have numbers in the opposition's last third, the defenders can find it difficult to get a good clearance on the ball.

This is when the ball can fall to your player 18-25 yards centrally out, in a prime position to take a shot.

Time and space for a shot can also be worked by playing a ball up to a centre forward around the box who releases it back for a midfielder to strike.

Just having players in the opponent's last third will lead, whether engineered or not, to chances to strike on goal from distance.

So encourage your players to shoot on sight. Then encourage them to shoot on target.

Striking the ball is a technical skill that also requires a cool head. Some players at lower level cannot kick a ball properly over distance as their set-up and execution is wrong.

Like a golf or tennis swing, a good contact requires a good balanced action through the ball. At local adult level, it may be *too late* to pick up the right technique if you don't have one, but a cool head can help.

Even those players that do have a nice strike of the ball can sabotage their own action if their mind isn't free and prepared to lead their body through the right measured steps.

Get your body over the ball, your momentum carrying through the strike, and concentrate on the quality of contact rather than the power of it.

Imagine you are taking a well-struck, whipped-in cross rather than a goal kick. Relax and let the body flow through the ball. Don't make panicky swipes at it. Keep your eye on the ball and concentrate on striking it cleanly and around its horizontal centre line.

If you aim at the goal as a general target and hit it cleanly, you will very often hit it straight at the keeper. He is the bull's-eye in your target. Do not be afraid to look up and choose the inside of a post as your bull's-eye.

It's all in the mind. Expect to strike it well. Visualise striking it well a split second before and let it flow, tracing the shape of your own vision.

On target and anything can happen.

The ball can slip through the smallest of gaps. Goalkeepers can, on occasion, let in the softest of shots and deflections are a constant source of goals. Bad conditions can make the ball slippery and difficult to catch. Hard and angled shots also provide follow-up opportunities for your teammates.

Therefore, if you are in the last third and a space in front appears, why not have a shot?

One-on-one

The closer you are to goal, the more chance you have of a successful strike on goal. One-on-one against the keeper has a very good chance of success.

It is therefore one of the most difficult attacks to mount, in that it attempts to go through the middle where the defensive spine is strong. It requires good vision and technical ability to set up.

A quick forward making well-timed runs and a skilful dribbler are perfect for this type of goal.

Once again, as in most soccer situations, **the key to getting one-on-one is movement**.

The quick forward should play on the shoulder of the central defenders. He should keep his eye on the defensive last man, as it is crucial that when his chance comes he is near enough to grasp it and still in an onside position.

A forward partnership (see chapter 6) should combine to create opportunities for the ball to be fed in behind the defence.

A midfielder in good possession of the ball in the attacking last third should be looking to thread a ball in behind the defence for either the quick loitering forward or the late run through from a fellow midfielder.

Good movement by the centre forward dropping off can enable these through-passes; dragging the centre halves just enough to leave an angle in behind them. **The run and the pass** then **need to be measured and matched**.

Good movement can also help a dribbler go one-on-one, dragging opponents away to leave a gap that he can wriggle through with the ball.

If defenders play a high line, looking for offside decisions, they are prone to conceding *one-on-one* type goals. A midfielder or defender with a good long-passing ability can suddenly get the chance to knock one over or past the defence and the quick (alert) forward can be in.

Once you get *one-on-one*, apply the finish; it is easy, you just have to score.

Good finishing is a mercurial talent. Strikers often have a preferred way of doing it.

When faced with the keeper narrowing the angle, some will blast it; some will chip it, place it or bend it round. Some like to take their chance early, others bluff and take their time.

Playing the percentage game, if it is at all within your control, is to quickly open the angle on the keeper, making him adjust his position and then quickly shooting against the direction of his movement. **Feinting to shoot is recommended** as a way of committing the keeper before you apply a well-placed finish.

Whatever they do, I think the best finishers do what comes naturally at the time. They *seem* not to worry about the occasion or game stand. They do not *appear* to entertain the negative thought or worry about missing.

Having no time to think may help. A goalie putting himself in no man's land has presented the finish to many a striker, relieving him of the mounting pressure.

One thing for sure is that **goal scoring, especially in a one-on-one situation, is a confidence thing**. If you have it in your head that you might miss, then you probably will. The power of negative thinking.

Missing chances comes as part of being a good goal scorer and should be shrugged off just as quickly as your last goal. They are history. Only the next chance counts.

Some players, no matter what their other qualities, have no confidence one-on-one and, short of seeing a psychologist, never will have.

It is just unfortunate if the player in question happens to be your quick centre forward.

Even good goal scorers go through their dry spells when every chance they seem to get is saved or struck wide. You cannot fix a confidence problem by shouting and moaning. You have to try to take the pressure from them.

You should be constantly doing this anyway, as restoring a player's confidence is harder than maintaining it on an ongoing basis.

A relaxed, confident striker should be scoring his one-on-ones as easily as he might do in training, head up and picking his spot.

The difference between training and match play is belief.

A tip is to say to yourself in conscious thought as you approach the goal, "I am going to score". In fact, every time you enter the box you should be saying to yourself, **"that ball is coming to me and I am going to score"**.

Once you have said it and visualised it, it is easier to do it. You are prepared for it. It is the power of positive thinking or "focus". Everything else is shut out. Not an option.

People and players are different, but the aim should be to get your striker to treat each chance in each game equally.

Do not go overboard about a goal or a miss, and do not excessively differentiate between one goal's importance or quality and another's.

The **pressure should be minimal and constant**, with plenty of goal scoring in training and encouragement being the main managerial tools.

A team with the right shape, passing the ball and moving its players properly within the team structure, will create goal-scoring opportunities.

"Keeping your shape" and "pass and move" are the two most important fundamental concepts in all levels of soccer.

Without these, you will have trouble moving players into the opponent's last third, with good ball possession. Therefore, you will have trouble scoring goals in open play.

"The long ball" is next and has its place in soccer as a way of getting players with good ball possession into the opponent's last third.

4

The Long Ball

To score goals, we need to get in to the attacking last third of the pitch.

One way of achieving this is with a long ball into the striker(s) around or in the attacking last third, with the midfielders following up in support.

The trouble with this is that most **central defenders thrive on intercepting this type of forward pass** and the striker(s) is outnumbered and can only gain and maintain possession a small percentage of times.

If the striker does gain immediate position his flick-on, layback, or attempt to hold up the ball is likely to go to the opposition, given the superior numbers the defending team has in this area of the pitch.

The hopeful punt into the attacking last third and the calculated long pass from defence to the forwards have their place in the game and no good team is shy to use them when called for. For these to work consistently, **you need a dominant target man and teammates available in support**.

The *teammates available in support* is the key to this. In a normal 4-4-2 set up, it is hard to get the midfielders and wingers up in support quick enough to allow the centre forward win a long ball and hopefully knock it off to his own team.

It requires midfielders with good lungpower and a centre forward with a good first touch, in the air as well as on the ground. Otherwise, it will be the opposition winning the majority of the first and the majority of the second stage of the long ball.

This tactic in normal play will usually mean giving possession away regularly, but remaining in **a strong team position to win it back and try it long again**.

It is a better tactic, for scoring goals, if you can **pack the opponent's last third** with your players. Obviously, this is not advisable in a normal starting set up.

Losing teams regularly use this tactic in the last 5-10 minutes of matches, often putting extra attackers up front to help win and maintain possession in this crucial last-third area.

The reason they adopt this tactic so late is because it is a high-risk strategy at both ends, in that the chances of both teams scoring is increased.

Some teams, who consider themselves technically inferior to their opposition or incapable, for one reason or another, of playing a passing game, adopt this tactic as *their preferred method* of getting into the attacking last third.

They consider it the strategy best suited to the strengths and weaknesses of their available players.

They may prefer to pack their defence and to concede the ball further forward rather than to risk losing possession, trying to build play in central or defensive areas of the pitch.

Such a team would characteristically have a defence-minded, non-ball-playing back four and a strong running midfield.

They should also have a dangerous forward who is capable of scoring via at least two of the three ways to score from open play. Someone who can be a threat with minimal support.

They can also hope that a long clearance or pass may eventually lead to a free kick, throw or corner from which a goal chance can be created via any of the three ways to score.

The long-ball team should concentrate on the many dead-ball situations, as if they want to compete using a long ball then they must cultivate an edge in this department.

The advantages of using the long ball as your favourite method for achieving the attacking last third may be seen in local soccer as follows:

The state of local-league pitches does not facilitate a slower build-up game.

The chances of getting the ball safely into the attacking last third by the long ball *really are better* than the slow build up.

The long ball can be pumped into the attacking last third of the pitch easily and often; and although possession is lost most of the time, it will provide goal opportunities.

The ball is bypassing the midfield, which would suit a team with technically poorer-quality players *than the opponent* in that area.

The long game can be tailored to suit your available players and can **hide deficiencies in technical quality**. Average players with *a good physical level and attitude* can carry it out. It requires the minimum of mental input. It is an easy concept to grasp.

The ball is lost primarily in the opposition's half, which means most of the now-defending team's players are goal-side of the ball at this time. This means a defence can be arranged using all outfield players. **A strong, anti-counter-attack set-up**.

Many goals are conceded through counter attack so this is a real bonus.

A long diagonal ball into the corners of the pitch will turn your opposition around and may enable you to get players a free ticket into the attacking last third. Especially if a throw-in is conceded. This tactic works in rugby and soccer alike.

A deliberate ploy is to play a few short maintenance passes around your full-back position and suck the opposition in numbers towards this area of the pitch, as they attempt to squeeze the ball and turn over possession.

The long diagonal ball is then played to **switch the play in one move** and hopefully isolate a defender against a forward on the other side of the pitch.

The timing and quality of this big switch-ball is crucial. One short pass too many and the chance may be lost and the ball turned over in a dangerous position.

The long ball can suit a big forward and a quick forward. If the big forward and the quick forward learn to read each other's game and work hard as a pair, it can be very effective.

The long punt as an emergency defensive necessity or via the goalkeeper is always part of the game. These moments are bound to arrive. So why not set up a team that can be very good at making the most of these long balls that arrive deep into the opposition's half?

In fact, why not set up a team to facilitate even more use of these long balls?

It provides chances in an unpredictable fashion, which can suit teams who struggle to create.

The long ball is simple and understood by all involved. If your team is physically stronger than the opposition, it is a way of using this size or strength advantage.

In my opinion, the long ball is best kept until 80-85 minutes of a more controlled soccer has proved fruitless.

When the need for a goal chance is desperate and you can place more players up in support of the forward ball, it can be very effective.

It should otherwise be used as an unexpected occasional weapon, the minority partner in the two ways of achieving the attacking last third of the pitch. The preferred way is "pass and move".

5

Goalkeepers

They are certainly a different breed to your average soccer player. In local league, they were traditionally big strong guys who did not like running around too much. They would often seem more suited to rugby than soccer.

The introduction of the pass-back law in the early nineties brought major problems to this type of goalkeeper. Suddenly he was expected to act like an outfield player in pass-back situations. This exposed many goalkeepers' lack of basic soccer skills.

Even under no pressure, kicking a moving ball proved beyond many.

Nowadays, goalies are much more likely to have decent soccer skills. Ability to *play on the deck* is now a recognised fundamental requirement for a good goalkeeper.

A goalkeeper is the focal point of a good defence. He is as likely to be the first line as the last line of that defence.

Good defenders, with a shaky goalie, are going to be shaky defenders. Shaky defending can often be saved by good goalkeeping. A defence can grow in confidence and ability when led and supported by a good goalkeeper.

A good goalkeeper, through his **calm decision-making**, his **unhesitant legwork** and **natural agility**, presents a massive hurdle to the attacking team, not only in the three ways to score from open play but in all dead-ball situations.

It helps if a keeper is tall, strong, brave and athletic with good footballing technical skills.

However, **good goalkeeping is largely about good decision-making**.

When to come and when to stay. Where to position yourself. Where to narrow the angle to make the target appear as small, whilst you appear as large as possible, to the opponent.

Deciding to use your legs, putting yourself in the right position before *committing to the save*. Conveniently, **most shots come straight at you when you are in the right position**.

Training drills and game practice all help a goalkeeper learn his task. Experience is a major factor and the best goalkeepers are often in their mid- and late-thirties.

Goalkeepers can play to an older age because less aerobic physical fitness is required, but also because **each match they play should improve their decision-making**. No position is as dependent on good decision-making as that of goalkeeper.

Experience can be the difference between making an easy save and having to make a fabulous save...or worse still, picking the ball out of the net.

Experience is often a euphemism for "reading the game" and making the right decision.

At local level, I would usually be happy if the keeper can kick a moving ball off the ground and out of his hands; that he saves all the easy ones and does not cause relatively harmless situations to lead to goal threats through bad decision-making.

I have seen goalkeepers in local leagues creating goals against from the most unlikely of situations, not to mention practically throwing them into their own net. This is, naturally, a big hindrance to winning a game.

These goalkeepers are often great shot stoppers, with cat-like reflexes. However, when the situation demands a bit of a **cool head, concentration and the right decision**, they are regularly found lacking. This becomes crucial in an important match.

A modern, decent goalkeeper would often come through the schoolboy system with all the basics in place. He would have all the mannerisms of a good goalkeeper, as seen week-in week-out on the television.

My main advice or focus when dealing with a goalkeeper before a match would be to **concentrate on the decision-making and the legwork**.

The worst scenario goalkeepers' face is being caught in "no man's land"; to be stranded in a position where he can no longer affect the game. Bad and hesitant decision-making is more often the cause of this.

There will always be the occasional, tempting, dangerous ball towards the goal that will demand from a goalkeeper quick movement, bravery and reflexes. Yet, 90 percent of what he has to do should be routine if his positioning and legwork are correct.

They will only be correct if his reading of the game, and hence decision-making, is correct.

Crosses. When to come and when to stay.

As a goalie, you can move forward quicker and easier than backwards, especially in a packed box. So have a starting position that favours covering the longer ball, having then to make a short forward run to deal with a shorter ball.

Come if you are sure you can get there and that either your own defenders or the opposition will not block your path (fairly).

If you do come, can you guarantee catching it? Or should you touch or punch it to a safe position? The ball can be like a *wet fish* to catch in bad conditions, so if under pressure it is often a better idea to punch.

If you do come, **take the ball at the highest point you safely can**. Since you can use your hands, this should ensure that any opposition is out-jumped.

Do not rush *silently* out and flatten your centre half who might be going for the same ball.

Do shout "keeper!" to warn your defence, to intimidate the opposition and alert the referee to protect you.

Do not come if your defenders can deal with it or if there is any doubt in your mind as to reaching the ball first and dealing with it adequately.

Do shout "away!" if there is any doubt as to whether you will come for the ball or not.

When in doubt, stay and protect your goal. We see many goals that might have been prevented had the goalkeeper decided to stay on or around his line. Stay and attempt to save any eventual goal strike. **The goal is your baby. Do not desert it easily**.

We can see with penalties how hard a goalkeeper can be to beat from 12 yards, with the striker under no pressure from defenders. So, "when in doubt protect your goal" is a massive piece of advice for a keeper to follow.

Through balls. When to come and when to stay.

You often see a goalkeeper dash off his line to confront an onrushing forward, only to be left stranded as the forward takes or strikes the ball into the unguarded net.

Usually there are defenders straining to get at the forward and if the goalkeeper had stayed, they would have got back and put the forward under enough pressure to affect his finishing.

The questions the goalie must ask himself in an instant are, can I get to the ball before the forward? If so, come for the ball. See the "sweeper" paragraphs below.

Can I get close enough that, although the forward may get the next touch, I will be so on top of him that the ball either should hit me or be forced too wide? Then come, but it's risky.

Will a defender get back in time to affect the striker's finish? Then stay.

The next question, in a one-on-one situation, is **how can he best put pressure on the forward?**

Forwards through on goal do feel the pressure. They are happy when the goalie makes up their minds for them by rushing into no man's land. Suddenly the pressure is off, as the striker's required finish is presented to him.

A glance at the onrushing keeper and at the roll off the ball will dictate to any decent striker the required finish: to chip or lob the goalkeeper into the unguarded net or bend the ball around him; to create an angle to stroke it past him or to take it past him using the momentum already gathered in his run.

The position the goalie should take up is almost a mathematical decision, as the example below might explain.

In training, you put a ball on the centre spot and ask a forward player at one end of the pitch, at the blow of a whistle, to run to the ball and score in the other end.

At the other end, you tell the goalkeeper on his line at the blow of the whistle to prevent a goal from the onrushing forward.

In this case, the forward might run the whole length of the pitch and the goalkeeper might have much more time than usual to get into position, but the key points of the match situation remain the same.

The goalie must decide if he can beat the forward in a 50-yard sprint to the ball. The answer is probably no. Now, where should he meet the forward so that he does not make up his mind for him and take the pressure off him by positioning himself in no man's land?

If he runs **out of his 18-yard box he becomes simply another outfield player** and is no longer permitted to use his hands. He cannot therefore dive as recklessly with his body at the forward's feet, as he might get away with inside his box.

If he runs out of his box, he leaves the opportunity open for the ball to be lifted over his head into the empty goal — a basic skill for any forward. The chance for the forward to open an angle for an easy pass into the unprotected goal is also increased.

The best place for the goalkeeper to meet the forward, if that forward has the ball perfectly under control, is actually around the 6-yard box using the 6-yard line as a positional guide.

Here he has reduced the chance of being chipped, as this is now a difficult skill for a forward, being closer to the goal. If the forward tries to improve his angle, the goalie, taking a couple of quick steps out towards the ball, will counter this, whereas it would take many more steps to do the same outside the 18-yard box.

The main thing he has done is remove the forward's soft options and put the pressure squarely onto the forward, who knows he should score but maybe has not yet decided how he is actually going to do so.

It has actually become a moving penalty situation, where the goalkeeper can start from his 6-yard line. If the forward takes an awkward touch as he enters into the 18-yard box, the goalkeeper can now attack the forward and pressure him into botching his finish.

This is exactly what should happen in a match scenario. The goalkeeper should make decisions which **remove the easy finishes for forwards**, so often provided by the bad decisions of goalkeepers.

As every second passes, the pressure on the forward mounts to make a decision and strike at goal. The possibility of missing enters his mind while he delays to see if the keeper has committed. The defenders also have more time and opportunity to recover the situation.

A goalkeeper will be presented with an onrushing forward in or outside the box in most games. It is a very common occurrence and one of our three ways to score in open play.

These **chances are often caused by a defence playing a high line**. In this case, and especially if offside is a deliberate ploy, the keeper should position himself accordingly and be ready to act as emergency sweeper.

These chances can also be caused if the central defenders mark too close, encouraging little balls in behind them or allowing the centre forward to turn them in one movement.

The keeper must keep an eye on this and be ready to rush out and claim or smother any ball that can be his, if committed to early enough.

You see countless easy finishes in these situations made possible by a goalkeeper deciding to put himself in no man's land or not coming when the ball would be clearly his.

That is why it is crucial to hammer home to your goalie the following points when the ball breaks behind his defence and suddenly a forward is through on goal.

If you cannot get to the ball first outside the 18-yard box, do not go for it, but stay and protect your goal starting from the 6-yard box. If you were on the edge of your 18-yard box, then backpedal to the 6-yard line to increase the pressure on the forward.

If you can get there first, then **do not hesitate** but **move quickly**, as some forwards can be deceptively fast when they sniff a goal chance.

Give your defenders a fair chance at getting back and upsetting the striker's finish. If the defenders look like putting in a challenge, **stand your ground around the 6-yard box** and prepare for whatever the outcome is.

Many a ball has trickled past a goalie who has committed himself too early, only to see a defender make a last-ditch challenge, resulting in a timid goal-ward bound strike that has him wrong-footed.

If the striker makes it into the box free of defenders, narrow as much angle as possible before the striker can attempt his finish, i.e. somewhere around the 6-yard box.

If you come out much further than the 6-yard box, it's hard to get your angles right without the benefit of the box line. You also have less time to react to the shot and have not significantly narrowed any more of the angle.

Stay on your feet for as long as possible and **make yourself large** to intimidate.

At the same time be ready, *if he makes a bad touch* and you suddenly get a chance at the ball, to move quickly forward. By suddenly shutting out all his angles around you and smothering the space in front of him, you can become the only target for the ball.

With one-on-one, as in most match situations, it is advisable to play the percentage game. Do the right thing, the percentage thing and you give yourself a great chance of coming out with the best result. **Give the forward a chance to miss**.

Using your legs

This book is not so much about the technical aspects of an individual's game, rather more about the mental aspects of the individual's role in the team. A goalkeeper will have many technical skills, which he will have developed over the years in training and during matches.

These technical skills, however, will only provide him with the means to carry out his decisions. If the decisions he makes are wrong, no matter how enormous his physical and technical skills might be, they will not compensate.

Connected to a goalkeeper's decision-making, I always believe, is the use of his legs in getting into the right positions to attack the ball or make a save.

I often see a weak-enough shot from 20 yards and further out float into the net, with the goalkeeper's despairing yet athletic dive falling short. He has dived too soon.

Two or three short, quick, backward or sideward steps on the way to the ball before the dive would have covered the distance required and given the dive the impetus necessary to reach the ball.

When a shot is just inside either post, it will be very difficult to save. The goal is a large area for a keeper to cover but with good footwork setting up a powerful dive, he may even be able to reach each post.

Some good goalkeepers scarcely dive at all in many games. Their expert reading of the game and quick feet to get them into perfect positions render diving unnecessary, except for the most challenging of goal strikes.

The goalkeeper must be ready to put in the quick paces that might be necessary during a game to prevent a goal situation developing or to make a save. He can help himself here by being poised on the balls of his feet whenever the ball is in his last third.

When it is closer, around the box, shifting his weight from one foot to another could help him keep his balance and prevent him being caught flat- or wrong-footed.

Goalkeeper as sweeper

A goalkeeper will be called on many times during a normal game to **intercept a ball played in behind his defenders**. He must be ready for this at all times, as he may only have a split second in which to decide if the ball will be his and where to meet it.

With the ball and a chasing forward moving towards you at pace, it is often very difficult for a keeper to decide whether he can wait for the ball to enter his 18-yard box and catch it before the arrival of the forward; or if he must leave his box and deal with it in an outfield fashion.

It is obviously better if he can **wait and catch it as soon as it enters his 18-yard box**.

My observation of good goalkeepers would be that they move up and down from the 6-yard box to the 18-yard box and outside, as dictated by the pattern of the game — this being the best position in which to react to a sudden through-ball.

It is also the best position for staying in communication with his defenders. The goalkeeper should be constantly warning them of dangers, such as forwards sneaking blindside of them.

In fact, a goalkeeper is perfectly positioned to **give defenders a constant running report** on things happening around them, e.g. whether they have time to take a touch, who they might have available to be passed to and who they should be marking.

They can and should be an extra pair of eyes for defenders in possession and defenders marking opposition.

The goalie should also advise them as to whether they should leave a ball for him or whether they should deal with it. However, he must also **listen to his centre half** and be ready to come out and collect the ball, under orders (centre half, captain or manager) if necessary.

This sounds like a massive contradiction, but is a crucial and common decision-making dilemma that faces the goalkeeper and his central defensive partnership.

Many times it is easier for a centre half to read that a dangerous forward ball from the opposition that beats the defence, chased by a speedy forward, will or will not go through to the goalie.

In this case, the centre half should alert the keeper to come for it. See also chapter 8, *Centre Halves*. The goalkeeper's narrow angle to the ball, relative to his distance from it, means that by the time the keeper has judged the speed of the ball and becomes spatially aware, the chance to come for that ball may be lost.

If the centre half says nothing and the keeper, assessing his chances, hesitates before deciding to come, he may be caught in the dreaded no man's land, as the forward reaches the ball first.

He may eventually decide not to come to a ball that was rightly his, if only he had recognised that fact in time. Then he must back on to his 6-yard box, the forward will be through and a one-on-one situation is caused.

The goalkeeper is part of a defensive team and it is important that the best decisions are made and communicated in the central defensive area, by whoever is in the best position to judge. Such calls to the keeper would normally be the remit of just one outfield player, the experienced last man and centre half.

The goalkeeper must **trust his centre half to warn him**, when the latter knows best.

The goalkeeper always has the last call on whether to come or stay for a ball. If he disagrees with the defender's call, he shouts back immediately "away!" and prepares to defend his goal, starting from the 6-yard line.

He may trust the defender implicitly for such calls and come as soon as called. If the call proves to be wrong, it is the centre half that bears the responsibility for it. He would soon be told to stop such calls, if they proved too often wrong.

The manager should decide on this. If a goalkeeper has a real decision-making weakness, it may be wise to take the pressure off him and instruct that *if* the captain/centre half calls him, he is to come immediately and claim the ball.

If there were no call (keeper!), he would have to make the decision himself anyway.

The call "keeper" is made when the centre half is sure that the keeper will reach the ball first to claim or clear. That is, if he comes immediately after the call. If he delays his decision, the chance will be gone.

If the call by the centre half to come is correct, the keeper should in theory be on his way to the ball anyway. His judgement has just been backed up by his centre half.

This is a contentious issue at local level and is hard to introduce to a goalie who is not used to it.

You definitely require an experienced centre half to make these calls and *only* when he knows best. All great defences use a complicated communication system, a shifting mix of hierarchical and consensual allocation of the important, goal-chance-saving decisions.

It means **the goalie is not alone in his decision-making**. Crucial goal-denying decisions are a *team* responsibility and the decision is made, naturally, by the most confident and convincing player. The defensive goal area is no place for shrinking violets.

I may have laboured this point! I am convinced that bad decision-making, in when to come and when to stay, is **a sign of bad communication between defence and goalie** and creates the largest amount of unnecessary goals you will see in the local game.

The most important conclusion here is that the goalkeeper commits instantly to one thing or the other. He either comes or he stays, but he never hesitates with his decision.

If he was undecided and gets a call to come, he has a split second to decide to come, (then quickly) or stay, (shout, "away!"). Under no circumstances should a goalkeeper half commit to coming for a ball or start too late. **When in doubt** (hesitation), **stay**.

After a period of mass defence, defenders can be slow to leave the box if the ball has been only partially cleared.

The keeper is in a good position to see this and should encourage them to "get out!" He keeps their defensive line as high as he can to put distance between the goal and the strikers and to give himself more space to claim as his own.

Distribution

A goalkeeper's ball-distribution talents are more and more in demand; keepers with an accurate pass or throw combined with a counter-attacking vision can **be a launch pad for attacks and goals**.

A goalkeeper who is happy with the ball at his feet can help maintain the ball for the curved back line. Whenever the last man is under pressure from the opposition and a square or forward pass is too risky, he knows he can turn around and play the goalkeeper.

The keeper is the constant, safe, out-pass for the central defenders. See pass-and-move chapter for **starting a move from the keeper**.

It is a massive confidence boost to any team at any level, when they know that passing back to their goalkeeper results in maintaining possession and more often than not provides the opportunity to build again, using the defensive curved line.

A winning team can also use up a lot of the opposition's time by passing back and often to a goalie with a cool head and good soccer skills. Most good goalies are expert at this, ball in play, legal time-wasting.

When the keeper intercepts a cross, free kick or corner he must be aware that the opponents have gambled a large part of their manpower on the success of these moves. The next few seconds provide a window of opportunity for him to **launch a counter attack**.

Before the interception is made, he must record in his mind the empty spaces on the field or likely teammates that will provide a quick out for him to begin a possible move.

Only then will he react perfectly to the actual situation, as soon as the ball hits his hands.

Goal kicks and kicks out of the hand are also constants in the game of a goalkeeper. These are skills acquired through natural talent and practice.

I would only suggest that since opposition central-defensive players are usually adept at winning long kicks directed at them — and unless you have an aerially dominant centre forward — that the kicks be aimed up one of the wings and at best be on an in- or out-swinging trajectory.

This should mean, at worst, if the opposition get a good clearance on it, the ball would be more likely to go behind your full back than behind your central defenders. If they get good hold of it on the wing, it is potentially less dangerous than in the middle.

We may **win more throws and therefore gain more possession** from opponent's clearances on the wings than from those in the middle. See chapter 12, *Throw-ins*.

Penalties

A penalty in normal play is nerve-wracking for the player taking it. If a goalkeeper stands his ground and does not commit to a side, I believe a lot of players panic and hit the ball too near to him and he saves it.

On the other hand, I have seen some tremendously important and incredible saves by a goalkeeper committing himself early to one side.

A save that would have been impossible from a delayed standing start.

Therefore, I would usually leave it up to the goalie on a one-off penalty to do what comes natural to him. However, penalty shootouts are a different matter.

In a penalty shootout, I maintain there are at least one, maybe two, saveable penalties. By that, I mean bad penalties. Penalties that can be saved from a standing start after waiting for the strike to be made before attempting to save it.

The pressure on penalty takers is huge and some, in their fear of missing the target, get too conservative with their strike or even strike it badly through nerves.

I also believe if the goalie stands his ground and does not commit, it upsets those penalty takers that like a goalie to start to a side before they decide which side to stick it.

They often have not decided on a plan B and when the keeper does not move, they suddenly realise they have not decided where to put the ball and panic with their strike.

The same goes for the people that try to blast the ball down the middle. Standing your ground definitely gives you a good shot at saving those ones.

Standing your ground, moving slightly to and fro on the line or favouring one side by a yard can all distract a nervous penalty taker. In this state, they can even miss the whole target.

In conclusion, I have seen too many saveable penalties go in after a goalkeeper has decided to gamble on a corner, that I can only recommend "save the bad ones" and stand your ground. The good ones can look after themselves.

If your goalie has good natural ability, he may have a chance even at saving those. He would certainly have no chance at them anyway if he gambled on the wrong side.

Reading the direction of the penalty by reading the body language of the player's run-up, planted foot or angle of the striking foot before ball impact is a talent that, even if it exists, cannot be conveyed in words. **Stand your ground. Save the bad ones.**

Standing your ground can be more difficult than it sounds. A penalty taker's body shape in his run-up can commit a goalie to one side, effectively wrong-footing him even if he intended to wait for the contact.

Again, shifting your weight from foot to foot during the run-up should help ignore the unbalancing effect of the body language in the taker's run-up.

Another aside to penalties during a match is why do players not involved stand on the edge of the 18-yard box and penalty arc?

They then have to start from a standing start to follow the ball in for any rebound. They should start from the same distance out as the taker's run-up and hit the 18-yard line or penalty arc at near full pace as the kick is taken.

A goalkeeper can have long periods of inactivity during a game, ended by sudden and very rapid strikes on his goal that require an instant decision and reaction on his part.

If the goalie is to be ready to make the right decision and use his legs to carry out that decision, he must be concentrated on the game at all times.

If he switches off at any point, he may find himself reacting to a sudden situation from the wrong starting position and eventually picking the ball out of the net. It is hard to make the right decision if you are not fully aware of the evolving situation.

Therefore, **concentration is a massive challenge for a goalkeeper**. I have often had to shout to a goalkeeper to "wake him up" in local soccer when I see he has taken up a bad starting position relative to the way play is developing; in other words, daydreaming.

If he doesn't concentrate, he won't be able to anticipate.

Mental imagery can be used by the goalkeeper to raise confidence and aid decision-making. This is especially useful in dead-ball situations, particularly edge-of-the-box free kicks.

He must visualise the possible shot or potential through ball or cross, and imagine himself dealing with it successfully. This aspect of "reading the game" can present him with the save or required response as the real action evolves.

The goalkeeper is the absolute last barrier to the opposition scoring a goal. A good goalkeeper will not alone make a winning team, but you will rarely find a team that can win big matches consistently without one.

The key to good goalkeeping is decision-making.

6

Strikers

Traditionally, *centre forwards* in a 4-4-2 were a unit. They came as a pair.

There was usually a big strong forward and a smaller quicker partner. The big forward would win the ball in the air and generally hold up or flick on passes to his teammate.

In the professional game the money and playing surfaces have improved and with these, the players, tactics and overall speed, if not also the standard of play. In line with this, the typical centre-forward partnership has evolved rather than changed completely.

Many teams now play a version of 4-5-1, which ensures a contested midfield in a style of game that suits the many passes of the modern professional game.

They often have one extremely athletic type as a kind of all-in-one; big man/little man combination. These athlete types are a relatively new addition to the game and are almost exclusive to the professional ranks.

However, **a good big one with a good little one up front will always prove a handful** and in the lower leagues not too much has changed.

Let us call the target man the number 9 and his striking partner the number 8.

Defenders generally dish out a bit of stick, but like most players they do not receive it too well. A centre forward who can occasionally bully his central defenders will always create opportunities for himself and his teammates.

For me, the ideal in local league would be that a **big centre forward leads the line**. He should contest balls with the opposing centre halves and attempt to hold up the ball.

If he cannot set up his partner straight away, he should try to play the ball safely back into his own midfielders.

His bread-and-butter job is to help his midfielders get into the last third with the ball in good possession. From the halfway line to just outside the opponent's box, **his job is ball winning and ball maintenance**.

He should be constantly timing runs off his central defender to provide a safe forward pass for his midfielder and full backs, or in order to create space for his number 8; the 9 showing to feet and the 8 running into the channels.

The 9 may need to move the centre half around, taking him slightly out of position by backing away before darting suddenly forward.

Timing his movement to match his teammates' ability to supply.

He constantly needs to be preparing these darts towards the ball, offering himself as an out pass by manipulating the centre half (the number 5).

Circling him, dragging him over to the sweeper-type centre half (the number 6), or towards the defending fullback. If he can get them to stand too close together, he will be creating a potential space elsewhere for his teammates to run into from deep.

There is always something he can be doing to help the team create.

Standing side-wards on, almost facing the marking centre half is a good way of keeping him in your view and not letting him surprise you with a challenge.

It is also a great way to receive the ball, the open body allowing you to turn easily.

The forward is then ready to pounce with his short run back towards the man on the ball *if* the situation presents itself. He will not always get a chance to make this move and even if he does, he will not always get the ball.

However, this is the bread-and-butter movement for this type of centre forward and movement is good for movement's sake. **His movement will create space for runs from deep**, if read and acted upon by his number 8, winger or playmaker.

The forwards are working an area dominated numerically by the opposition.

They have to create space so that the ball can be safely played up to them and others, otherwise the defence will read and pick up any forward passes or deter them from even being made.

The forwards should try and stretch the play, forcing the defenders back to cover their movement. This will make it easier for balls to be played up to them and into space, from the back. The defenders will try and hold a line which only well timed movement will dissolve.

Standing still because you are marked is not an option.

The 9 may just recycle a received pass back into the midfield, but in so doing these ball- maintenance passes edge the midfield up, into the opponent's last third, where the three ways to score in open play occur.

See the pass-and-move chapter for the importance of good movement in order to progress midfielders into the attacking last third.

Gaining ball possession — and the maintenance of same — is a busy job for the main number-9-type centre forward.

If he can win possession in the opponent's half, provide a safe forward outlet pass and maintain possession he is doing his primary job; his outside-the-box job.

If, as a local manager, I had a suitable number-9-type player I would seek to drum into him **the need to win and maintain possession**. He is doing it deep in enemy territory so it may be more difficult, but the potential reward for him, is a goal chance.

He must be aware that simply to get a controlled ball up to him, the team has done well. He should not waste this possession lightly by trying high-risk passes or attempts to turn.

With our **centre halves dropping deep and the strikers pushing the opponents back**, we have provided a situation where the central midfielders have the space and therefore time to start moves which can create genuinely *planned* attacking opportunities.

A normal situation may be that the two forwards are square to each other, 20-25 yards apart around the attacking last third. The midfielder on the ball is ready to pass and the number 9 darts suddenly towards the ball, bringing with him his centre half, the number 5.

His fellow forward, the 8, now times his diagonal run into the space vacated/created by his companion number 9 and centre half marker, number 5.

A steep midfield pass ignores the possession-maintenance offer of the number 9; and if the fellow centre half, 6, has not pushed out, creating the perfect offside trap, the 8 may then bend his run and be through toward goal.

Basically, if one forward, the 9, is coming short, showing and competing for the ball to help the midfield and full backs progress up the park, his partner, the 8, should be staying long. He has to keep the pitch stretched. In fact, he should be making longer cross or diagonal runs timed to complement the short pass offer of the number 9.

As manager, you should hardly see the *actual number* 9 on the back of the shirt unless it is in the box. You should see lots of the *number* 8 running away into the attacking last third.

The evolved variation on this and a very common move in good football anywhere on the pitch is the "**third man running**". This combines the movements of a unit to set a man free.

An example of this is where the number 9 comes short with his back to goal, receives the ball and *plays it directly back* to a midfielder who is ready to play it first time.

Meanwhile, the 8, starting his run as the ball is laid up to the 9, has timed his square-cross run to bend through a gap *just as the midfielder slips the ball first time* into that gap.

The "third man" effectively appears from nowhere to be the main recipient of the move.

This could also be a winger or full back suddenly scampering up the line, starting as the centre forward receives it and in full flight as the midfielder passes into the desired space.

The *third man's run* is too late to receive the first pass and is clearly not the object of the backward second pass. Because of this, the start of his run and its significance is missed.

When the third pass comes, it can be too late for a ball-watching opponent to react and block — simpler than it might sound on paper and very effective.

At lower local level, we tend to make our moves in isolation, rarely in combination. Teammates don't play with joined-up thinking, when just a little of it would do so much for our creativity and ultimately game enjoyment.

This secondary running, which involves taking planned advantage of an immediately previous diversionary or set-up move is a role suited to the more mobile, quicker forward, the number 8.

Well-timed movement at pace will always unlock a team's defences.

His range is the length of the opposition's back four, but his eye is firmly on making sudden, darting, often angled runs behind the two central defenders.

He is constantly on the move or ready to move, **constantly looking for a good starting point** from which to launch his move.

Runs across the defensive line open a wider angle for the midfielders to hit, giving them more time for the pass and a larger margin for error. The bigger angle takes longer to run through. Steep runs present a narrow and fleeting angle that is much more difficult to hit.

Diagonal and square runs, timed to bend, are perfect for steep passes.

The 8 must stage his moves if they are not to be predictable and momentum-less. You move out of a space to run into that same space.

You have to go out to go in. You pull out wide to start a run back across a defensive line that can then be bent in, as the ball is played.

The 8 times his movement (reading the game) so that he can jump on any chance of a ball appearing behind the defensive line. If he reads his partner well, he will know what types of passes the number 9 makes and will be ready for his flick-on.

He will not be too close or too far apart, *when it matters*. He must be ready to exploit any good play or movement from his number 9.

A crossover run, in which they simply swap positions, may be enough to get one of them on the ball. Runs again should be timed to suit the provider.

In order for many runs to work, apart from their timing, their **starting positions need to be staged**.

Go long and spin to get the ball short. Go short and spin to get the ball long.

The 8 should drift away from the 9, along the defensive last line, as if looking for the very common local league over-the-top steep or diagonal ball.

He then times his move across the back four, speeding up and ready to bend his run as the space emerges. He must work on **drifting away into a good starting position**, from which his "joining in" runs can be launched.

This number 8 should **play on the shoulder of the last man**.

He has to, because part of **his job is pushing the opponent's defensive line back**.

This means he plays on the edge of being offside. He must be constantly aware of the defenders stepping up, opening his body to look square along the line, **adjusting his position crab-like to stay onside**, preparing for his moment to time and bend a run.

In local football, the ball *unexpectedly* gets past the centre halves without any creation necessary. A centre forward playing on the last man would be through on goal.

This happens regularly in local standard games. It can be the result of the defenders playing too high a line, combined with weak control, a bad back pass or a deflected ball.

It is a shame to let it go unpunished, because both forwards have come short, instead of one of them waiting for that exact opportunity that we know will come and come again.

Therefore, I would try to get over to my two centre forwards a mental visualisation of the type of things they should be trying to do or expecting to have to do during a match.

The number-9-type may have to hold the ball up and maintain possession before being able to play it back out to the wings or midfield.

He may have to back in to a defender when necessary to claim a ball.

Keeping his body at an angle between the opponent and the ball. Shielding the ball on his outside foot, using strong arms, kept wide and low.

Widening his stance and bending his knees to root the ground as he feels the opponent's challenge. Leaning his weight towards his centre half to prevent being knocked off balance. No straight locked legs but bent knees, balanced and primed to push off, at pace.

When he has no first-time pass option, he must turn sideways on so that he can keep the defender away with a strong arm, body and legs between him and the ball. He maintains touch contact with him to keep the ball out of his reach.

The 9 must be able to shield a ball this way so that he can turn away in either direction if the defender attempts to come round and dispossess him.

If he can, he should receive the ball with an open body so that he can turn an opponent if he gets too close or at least trap the ball into a more favourable direction.

He must expect to have to meet the pass, taking the space to the ball before the centre half claims it. He cannot only be available for the perfectly weighted ball.

He should pressure the centre halves into losing the ball and give them no easy headers; at least attempt to jump with them and knock them in the air (legally). He should flick on balls he cannot control back into his midfield or forward, hoping to find his partner.

He should focus on his movement, **concentrating on timing his runs** to match the delivery. Matching his availability to the possibility of supply.

Pushing the centre halves back by moving constantly behind and between them, before darting in front to be first to any balls played forward.

Making clever little runs behind them, runs that they feel obliged to cover, creating room in midfield for his team to play.

He makes one move for the defender and one for himself, taking them or their interest away from the space he covets; timing his own dart into that space for the arrival of the ball.

It is advisable, occasionally, for the big man to stand on the smaller, sweeper-type centre half, who ideally has his sights on the number-8-type forward. This drives the centre halves too close to each other or forces the sweeper to take up a different position.

The number 9 has to **keep the centre halves busy** thinking about and countering his movement. If he allows them to concentrate on the ball too much, they will have an easy afternoon intercepting it.

He has to make sure he is in the box as much as possible when there is the possibility of a cross coming in. It is a bonus if this target-man-type of forward is a prolific goal scorer.

The number-8-type should **be constantly on the move along the length of the back line**. He should be looking along the line to check and keep himself onside.

He must have an eye on his number 9's movement, ready to dash into any space vacated/created by him. There is no use in the 9 creating space if the 8 is too far away to take advantage of it; or even worse and harder to fix, he is unaware of its creation.

He is looking out to see if a midfielder can slot a ball through the gaps between the four defenders. **His job is to provide penetration into the last third**, beyond the first defensive line. Intelligently angled and timed runs with an injection of pace *will lose* his marker.

If he sees the possibility of a flick on by his partner or a pass through a gap, he should angle and time his run so that he is onside and has some momentum to steepen his run past the defenders, as the ball is played.

He too should make sure he is hitting the box at the first hint of a cross coming in. Being more mobile than his number 9, he could choose to make his runs into the box across the defenders to the near post, leaving the far post for the 9 and the other winger.

Sometimes, a dummy run away from the near post and then back may be necessary to strand the defender. The timing of these runs is key. The attackers should expect the best and be speculative in their runs into the box.

If a cross is coming into the box, say from the right wing, you might enter the box through the middle, being well marked. You can then speed up your run, threatening to pass behind your marker's back and head for the far post.

When you get him turned slightly to cover this move you can quickly cut across him, head for the near post and be first to the cross.

This **getting across your defender in the box leads to many goals**. It can happen unprepared by any dummy run, if your marker is ball-watching or has set himself up at a bad angle to you. He will not see your blindside move until it is too late.

You still have to time your movements to the cross. This timing should come naturally *to an experienced striker*, so long as he is up to the pace of the game.

Being in the right place at the right time is the striker's reward for reading the game and his application of soccer knowledge.

Be ready for your chance, be calm and **expect to score**.

Be prepared to miss and pay it no attention, but don't be afraid to miss. A goal scorer needs to nurture his own confidence and psychology for this.

The concentration and awareness necessary to make good runs can be learnt and encouraged. The occasional reminder from the bench to "be sharp" accompanied by a finger tap to the temple can waken up a forward who has shut down the brain and gone on automatic pilot.

The number-8-type forward should study the opposition's offside trap and use it to his advantage.

He should learn when to take a man on and when to pass the ball; when to shoot and when to try and set up a better-placed teammate.

If he decides to shoot, it should often be with his team game in mind. He should get it on target and shoot across the goalkeeper, to the far post, so that his team may benefit from rebounds.

When to shoot and when to dummy-to-shoot, to create an even better shooting opportunity.

The dummy-to-shoot is one of the easiest and most effective dribbling moves in the business. No forward should be without it. You think you're panicking...imagine what the defenders are doing.

As always in life, there is the equally valid contradictory statement. A forward should also know when to **pull the trigger**. Sometimes you only get one chance.

A good player will recognise when to shoot, when he should take his shot early and when he can feint to do so. **Decisions make the difference in all positions**.

He should love playing on the last man and really come alive in the attacking last third.

Above all, he should **love to score goals**, all types of goals, whatever their importance and whoever the opposition. Ideally, he should be good at it as well.

Both forwards should be keenly aware that when the team has entered the last attacking third, with the ball in good possession, the concept of the three ways to score in open play takes on high-priority significance.

Every move should be one that increases the team's chances of scoring. Their sole thought should be to help create and finish one of the three ways.

In defensive mode, their main job is to harass and restrict the opponent's back line. They are the first line of defence and should take their lead from their central midfielders.

They must try to stop the back line switching play easily across the pitch or passing them out of the game. They must work together to press successfully.

They should direct the opposition play into safe areas of the pitch, where their team is set up ready and waiting for them.

They may need to drop back in order to do so. See chapter 7, *Centre Midfielders*, for defence tactics.

7

Centre Midfielders

The central-midfield unit works as a pair; in our 4-4-2 template it consists of a defensive holding type and an attacking playmaker type.

They are the hub in the machine. They **link the other positions and tasks together** and are key players in controlling possession of the ball and the direction of the game.

They, like the other central units, combine better as a pair with differing physical and technical attributes. At lower local-league level, as in all its central partnerships, a mix of youth and experience is often the best combination.

The older playmaker can read the game and pick a pass, but may not have the change of pace to make runs past people or into the box; the younger playmaker can use wall passes, dribbles and darting runs to help his forwards create.

The holding-type playmaker would typically be a physically strong ball winner and an effective short and long passer.

The creative playmaker, number 10 normally, would be a quicker and more adept ball carrier with an eye for gaps in the opposition and the killer pass.

More importantly, **they are both playmakers**.

They both need to play with their heads up and be comfortable on the ball. **They both need to be aware of and maintain a triangle of outlet passes around them at all times** when looking for and when in possession.

This means they have to assess things early. To do this, you need good information. To have that, you need good communication.

You need to play with your body open to the play and your head up and swivelling so that your game radar is totally switched on, with no blind spots.

Since they are the hub and the ball flows through them into the other positions, it is necessary that the ball does not get *too frequently delayed or lost* in their positions.

A central midfielder must be *available and able* to **receive and keep the ball under pressure**. He should try and receive the ball at an angle, whether played up to him from behind or back to him from in front.

This means **he constantly works on his starting position**, relevant to the developing play.

Only then can he consistently play side-on with his body open, which is the sign of a good midfield player. From this position, he is already half turned to evade danger or half turned to exploit an open space or pick his next pass.

If you receive the ball with an open body, your opponent will not know which way you mean to turn and will hesitate to rush in, for fear of being beaten. This enables you to turn away, keeping the ball on the far side of the adversary.

At lower local-league level, we receive the ball either with our back or our front square to the opponent. He knows exactly our options and will rush in to dispossess us.

Side-on, you are also in a good position to shield the ball — **a very necessary skill if pass- and-move is to succeed under pressure**.

This skill is largely missing at our lower level, so how and why a player should shield the ball are worth noting here.

The midfielder should keep his body at an angle to, and between, the opponent and the ball.

If under pressure, shielding the ball on his outside foot, using strong arms, kept wide and low. Widening his stance and bending his knees to root the ground as he feels the opponent's challenge. Leaning his weight towards his marker to prevent being knocked off balance. No straight locked legs but bent knees, balanced and primed to push off, at pace.

Ready to turn away from, or past, a presser who has been sucked in too close, on what is now *the wrong* side. Simultaneously holding his presser off and getting his head up, so that he can successfully and calmly pick a safe out pass.

Without this skill you may have to play with blinkers, forced to go forward quickly every time.

With this skill you maintain possession, you buy time for your teammates to open an angle, you make space for yourself to lift your head and you create your own possibility of a 360- degree passing range.

Then you can rightly be considered the hub of the team.

Defending

The central midfielders are in a perfect position to marshal the team's defence in the first stages of the opposition's possession. Therefore, much of this book's defensive observations now follow.

Between themselves and their centre halves, they should boss the rest of the team in their defensive duties; and ensure that **the ball is pressured in units of two or three players** in each of the areas where the opposition are seeking to gain ground.

Other players must avoid being sucked in to these areas because if the ball is successfully switched, you will find yourself short elsewhere.

They must ensure the **defending is done on a team and not an individual basis**.

The actions of the central midfield depend on the nature of the team's defensive strategy.

High-pressure (think Barcelona) or low-pressure (think Italian) defending.

High pressure requires hard work from all to deny time and space *as soon as* the ball is lost. It attempts to win the ball back before the opponents can establish a good possession of it.

Low pressure delays an immediate concerted press on the ball and concentrates first on getting everyone safely back into position.

High pressure is high risk as you squeeze the ball high up the pitch, in numbers, shutting down all adjacent space but leaving large pockets of space elsewhere *if the opponent successfully evades* your press.

Low-pressure defending reduces the space available in the *most dangerous areas* by getting set up first behind the ball.

Conceding immediate possession and space around the ball in order to restrict it later on, where it matters.

Changing to high pressure, through necessity, if the opponents and the ball reach your defensive last third. In the last third, low-pressure defence should not exist.

High pressure requires a superior fitness level and teamwork. You can win the ball back quickly and high up the pitch, which is obviously a good thing if successful. At certain points in a match it may be worth the risk and if losing late on, it is unavoidable.

Low-pressure defending, where you delay the move and jockey back into position, would be more suited to general play and to lower-league fitness levels. It also requires less precision, in terms of communication skills and the timing of the team work.

High pressure seems to be the future of high-level football, with the Spanish leading the charge. Our level is not fit enough or synchronised in its play enough for that.

We also do not get the opportunity, if our opposition do not build from the back. Even presuming they do, and that is exactly what I am advocating they should do, it would seem **low-pressure defending suits low-level soccer**.

Defending starts from the front. Alas, many forwards need to be reminded of this continually and ball-watching is the enemy of good defending, anywhere on the pitch.

The opposition's back four will seek to advance up the pitch whilst maintaining possession; and the first thing the midfielders should organise is the strikers' and wingers' defensive tactics.

The two forwards and at most, one winger, should only ever be tempted to squeeze onto the opponent's defensive line in good possession, in their last third, when they have spotted a definite opportunity to turn the ball over.

A chance, usually the result of hesitation, bad control or lack of pass options in that back line possession.

If **one decides to squeeze, then they must all commit to do so**, quickly closing down the ball and available outlets.

Unless desperately chasing a deficit, in all other cases they should drop back to just short of the halfway line before applying a synchronised press of the ball.

Never mind the ball, get on with the game.

You need to avoid a forced squeezing of the ball in high areas by just one or two players, as they will prove easily bypassed and left stranded.

That would allow the first phase of the opposition's possession to be too easily achieved and may require a central midfielder to confront an advancing centre half or full back.

This inopportune forced pressure on the ball by your forwards can lead to a defender running freely through the midfield and gives your opponents impetus, even numerical advantage, in a move you never quite catch up with.

If ball possession is lost whilst attacking the box or last third in number, you may have a **counter-attack situation** where the opponents speed up their forward play, taking advantage of the sudden space open to them.

In all open play, the holding midfielder and available defenders should always have an eye to providing cover for full backs and wingers that have made runs up front.

Pre-empting a problem and being there to solve it, before it becomes one.

If a break is successfully launched, the holding player must prioritise and track the central run with the ball by the opposition, passing him on, using good communication with his available defenders as necessary.

This is where a centre half making a brave and correct decision not to back off, moving quickly out into the midfield, can snuff-out a counter attack before it becomes too late.

The midfielder should run in behind him, providing cover in a reversal of positions for the sake of the team, in that specific defensive instance. As ever, decision-making is key.

In this counter-attack situation the remaining full back also moves to a central position, focussing on defending a direct goal threat. A compact defence at the attacker's preferred entry point can make up for a lack in numbers.

The first duty in defensive transition for those caught wrong-side is to get back behind the ball, especially compact through the middle, *the quickest route to your goal*. At least one player who is goal-side should confront any advancing ball carrier.

Any remaining defenders must contain the movement of the counter attackers, using the offside rule as an aid and strength in the middle to force the attackers wide.

If you are slow or disorganised in changing from attack to defence, you may pay the price. The opposition will attack rapidly into the available spaces deep inside your ranks.

Drop quickly back, denying these spaces to them before energetically squeezing in units of two, three and four — not high up and in isolation.

The centre halves and defensive midfielder must be thinking of a possible turnover of the ball when the rest are attacking the opponent's last third. Only then will they be ready to manage the transition and deal with the counter attack.

Concentration at all times. **Good defensive players expect the worst**.

It is the central midfielder's task to make sure you routinely get back as a team into a solid defensive shape before you tackle as a team, not committing yourselves one by one.

In normal play, you have to press the opposition in midfield, getting close and in their face, cutting off their options and isolating them on the ball. You cannot let them play around you, as if you were statues.

You also cannot challenge them, as if you were villains in a bad action movie, each having a go, one by one. Winning the ball is a team skill as much as an individual one.

A good unit of **first defence is one player to pressurise** and try to win the ball or force the move away from a vulnerable area. He jockeys unless and until he has support.

One player in support in case the first gets beaten, thus allowing the first to make a responsible challenge. He also further hems in and restricts the short passes or the angle of attack available to the opponent in possession.

Another player, acting as cover, tracking the runner anticipating a medium-length ball out from this position into a danger area.

The rest of the team contract onto their opponents according to where they are, but always with a first thought as to where their *goal* is — the main *object* of their defence.

The central midfielder, marshalling this initial defence, should have a clear idea of what the opposition are trying to do and therefore the steps to be taken to deny them.

The object for the opposition is to get into your defensive last third, with the ball in good possession, so as to construct a goal chance through the three ways to score in open play.

In the second phase of the opposition's possession, your defence may have retreated to their natural first defensive line. That is protecting the entrance to the last third.

With the ball being played now in your half of the pitch, you should still have your midfield bank of four, containing any attempts by their midfield to break this line.

Your centre forwards should be deterring the opposition centre halves from positively engaging in possession maintenance.

This is a very solid defensive structure and the attacking team will find it difficult to break through without very good individual penetration or excellent passing and movement.

If it is real backs-to-the wall or final minutes' defending, protecting a result, then two banks of five may be the policy.

Using low-pressure defending, many professional teams are happy to let the opposition pass the ball around the opponent's back four, and in and out of the opponent's midfield.

As long as the ball remains at least between and, even better, in front of their own two defensive lines of four and definitely in front of their defensive last third.

So long as the two lines of four **do not drop prematurely deep** or show no sign of moving back up the pitch when possession is won or as attacking moves are repulsed.

The two flat lines of four is evidence that the team understands good defence, is not as much about seeking one-to-one confrontation, tackling and ball-winning as it is about stopping the opposition team from doing what it wants to do.

This structure of two banks of four, defending the last third line with synchronised pressing, will win more possession through timely interceptions of poor passes, careless play and ball control than through looking to force ball-winning challenges.

A clever midfielder intercepts many more balls than he wins in tackles. Reading your opponent's intent is a skill more valuable than a hard last-ditch tackle. This doesn't negate the need for well placed aggression in midfield; it just favours brain over brawn.

The two flat lines of four merge and distort in response to the attackers' movement, as units of players squeeze the ball together, suffocating the space as the ball is played in amongst them.

It is important that only two or three players pressure the immediate space around the ball and that the others maintain discipline, awaiting their turn to become a coordinated unit of ball pressers, should the attack switch into their area.

If the ball or move is repelled, the flat line is resumed, ready for a new squeeze onto and around the new opponent in possession as alternative attacking moves are launched.

These two flat defensive lines are ready to expand, moving out quickly into two arc-shaped attacking lines the moment possession is won.

You do not want to be *playing in and around your own last third* for any prolonged period. If you do, you are very likely to concede a goal.

If the defensive last third is breached, the situation becomes more critical.

The midfielder must stick with the runner and cannot be left flat-footed after trying to intercept a one-two. You must not ball-watch and let your opponent run, but must react more in a basketball fashion, concerned with your opponent rather than the ball.

The central midfielder has to track or pass on through immediate communication any of the opposition midfield's sudden penetrating runs. The centre halves will be busy containing the forwards and will be undone by a run from deep, unless alerted or abetted.

Within the defensive last third, closer marking is required that will lead to challenges and tackles needing to be won.

Touch-tight marking, the closing down of defensive gaps, covering runs and blocking or preventing shooting opportunities are unavoidable if goal chances are to be denied.

When the game has filtered down to this individual contest, it is up to the individuals on your team to show their quality and decision-making on an individual level.

I have no theory for *individual* defensive talent that translates reliably in practise. To me, it appears an innate talent for reading the game from a defensive viewpoint and a natural desire to **compete for and win the ball**.

When the pressure is on and the ball and opposition are hitting the 18-yard box, it is the quality of your defence-minded players that will decide the day.

The central midfielders cannot drop too deep or stand off their opponents around the edge of the box. If they do, these may shoot or play a controlled pass into your 18-yard box that undoes your centre halves.

The structure of two banks of four is also perfectly set up for **counter attack as soon as possession is won**.

It is vital that "possession is won" is recognised correctly and not prematurely.

Playing pass-and-move around your own *congested* last third is not to be taken lightly.

More often than not, it will be advisable to clear your lines with a long ball up front or out of play; *staging a retaking of the defensive last third line*, by advancing quickly behind this ball.

The pass-and-move game is always safer if started from outside the defensive last third line, and especially so if there are still opponents in it from a repulsed attack.

Safest is when possession is won in your opposition half, with the team already well distributed and far enough up the pitch. This could arise simply from a throw-in, free or goal kick.

Having won the ball here, you can now **play the ball backwards into safe possession** using your back line that is now spread out and numerically dominant in your own half.

This is a much safer place to start the pass-and-move game, probing for gaps to attack.

However, **if good possession is won in your last third** and it *is feasible* to pass or run your way out of this area, then it would be *bad play* to squander this chance of counter attack by booting the ball out of touch or aimlessly up front. Decisions, decisions.

Players must not live in the past but must live in the moment, reacting to an opportunity to attack even if it arrives at the height of a period of desperate defence.

Winning the ball in your 18-yard box and expanding rapidly out, whilst staying in control of the ball, can catch the attacking team seriously out of position.

It is when the attacking team enters your defensive third in open play, sensing a goal chance, that they attempt their most speculative runs and take up intuitive and disjointed positions that can be broken through with one decisive interception.

They are at their most vulnerable when committed in numbers to attacking the box and a good pass, run or dribble, after an interception, can catch them on the wrong foot and create a break into their defensive last third.

A break into their defensive last third, without them having had the opportunity to stage a measured retreat into it.

This is more likely to happen to a team desperately chasing a deficit, but does happen to a team not cautious enough in attack or prudent enough in defence. And also, of course — and why the game is so unattainably beautiful — through sheer attacking bad luck.

If this should happen to your team, you must hope that a full back and any central defence maintain their composure and *combine centrally to jockey, divert or otherwise delay the counter* so that enough of the team can get back before a goal chance can be created.

Many goals in open play, at all levels, arise through a bad **transition from attack to defence**. Attacking corners and prolonged forays into the attacking last third can, through sudden ball loss, put your team in mortal danger of conceding.

Conversely, mounting a fast and accurate **attacking transition out of defence** is a regular source of goals.

Be prepared to **do both things well**, as they are a constant in the game.

Attacking

I advise that players should count the number of times they give away *good possession* in a game. Even forwards who play in more high-risk areas of the pitch should do so.

Every time they lose possession in one of these *unforced error* moments, it should feel like a loss in the family.

How many times do I see a player constantly leaking the ball to the opposition and seeming not to notice? Usually because in his mind, it was *nearly* a successful forward pass.

In lower league, anybody in any of the positions *needlessly giving the ball away* grabs my attention as a possible liability. He would have to be doing something else for me very well, if this constant conceding of good possession was to be tolerated.

You should aim to count the moments in a game where you patently did the wrong thing or negligently conceded possession on one hand.

Who surrenders the ball meekly and **who keeps it, is never a bad judge of who is helping your team create** and who is a weak link, effectively playing at times for the opposition.

Central midfield is not a place for players who squander possession.

They are the distribution centre and key to the pass-and-move and possession-maintenance systems that allow the team to progress, whilst maintaining its shape, into the attacking last third — where the goals come from.

The two central midfielders should not get too close to each other at the start of possession. They are harder for the opposition to contain when the distances between them are constantly changing as their paths cross, creating space for each other.

They must be able to pass to each other regularly by opening angles and making short runs. Give-and-go wall passes are their stock in trade.

Quick thinking and alert, often disguising the intent or object of their pass. Moving blindside as opposition eyes follow the ball.

The holding and playmaker title would suggest that there is a certain **depth to their positions** and this is more apparent the further they get up the pitch, and especially so in the attacking last third.

This diamond shape with the wingers allows the attacking midfielder to make daring forward runs into any space left by the opposition.

The number 10 makes a 10 to 20-yard run out of the curved middle line to create space or receive the ball and with the help of the forwards, edges the midfield line up behind him; pushing the opponent's defensive line back, as they cover forward movement from the wingers and strikers.

The 10 playmaker is much freer to speculate in his movement and passing. He will make penetrating runs ahead of the ball, helping to stretch the play.

The holder operates almost exclusively in the central area, staying behind the level of the ball and his passing is more conservative.

The holding player is constantly recycling the ball out to the wings and back into his defence, abandoning one attacking move before the ball is lost, so that a new one can be started.

His prime objective is to maintain possession and his tool for this is his constant use of maintenance and safe out passes.

He seeks out the creative players, the wingers, forwards and playmaker whenever it is safe to do so. He looks to play the ball into the forwards' feet to move the team the next rung up.

He looks out for the **third man running** as he receives the ball back from a striker, hoping to play a pass first time to the other forward or a winger making a sudden burst into space.

When it does not appear safe, he recycles the move, starting again rather than risk losing the ball. **He dictates the steady rhythm of the game.**

He supports the playmaker, opening angles to provide a safe out for him so that the number 10 can probe the defences, knowing that if he stops, shields the ball and looks up the holding midfield player will be available for him.

The 10 will create space by making a bursting run into an area with the ball and then having drawn the opposition to him, check and quickly reverse-pass the ball out of this area, switching the angle of attack, hoping to catch the opponents light somewhere else.

When the opportunity presents itself, the 10 playmaker will make his penetrating run or pass deep into the attacking last third. **Unexpectedly upping the tempo**. Driving in behind the defence. With and without the ball.

Using one-touch and wall passes, he will prove as elusive as dust to mark, creating instant angles for himself on the ball, from within which to slip a killer pass.

Otherwise, he will use his holding companion and full backs as a regular safe out pass, preferring also to await his chance rather than force the play.

The central midfielders are thus always aware of each other's position.

This is even more important when the holding and playmaker roles are interchangeable. They must not both get caught ahead of the ball in the attacking last third in case it is lost. They should not be found together out on the wings.

The geographic central midfield position should effectively never be left vacant.

I'm not saying the holding player doesn't go forward, but he has one eye on legging it back as soon as it breaks down. So a good holding midfielder runs 20 yards back, repositioning himself, whilst the opposition are still thinking how to attack.

The *three ways to score* should be uppermost in a central midfielder's mind when in both last thirds of the pitch.

They should be looking for a chance **to shoot** whenever the ball might fall to them within the attacking last third.

They should keep their eyes on the movement of the forwards, as they may just get a split second to play a pass at a well-timed run.

They should be **looking for gaps through the defence** where a pass or a dribbling run can be made to force a one-on-one against the keeper.

They should also be getting the ball out to the wings as **crosses lead to goals**.

The 10 playmaker should join the forwards attacking these crosses by making late runs into the 18-yard box whilst the holder hovers ten yards outside.

If there is no chance to execute any of the three ways to score in open play, then ball-maintenance passes should be employed until there is an opportunity.

A little patience is a good thing.

Life and soccer are full of contradictions and decision-making dilemmas. **Don't over pass.**

Take your opportunity to shoot, cross or one-on-one as soon as it presents itself. Do not wait for better occasions, as they are unlikely to appear. *A bird in the hand is worth two in the bush.*

Local level is not meant to emulate Barcelona, but players have to **have the courage to play some keep ball during the game** and not just in training.

Courage is not just putting your head in amongst the feet or your body on the line. Courage is also putting your foot on the ball and getting your head up, daring to pass and move.

Keeping the ball in the attacking last third encourages more of your players into this area. That will increase the chances of creating one of the three ways to score.

Patient passing will encourage the opponents to drop their guard as the concentration necessary to assess and cover all the movement ahead and around them is used up, little by little, with each pass. Panic and desperation can ensue in a team under sustained pressure.

If you win the ball in your own defensive third after being under sustained pressure, you may find the opposition exposed in numbers at the back.

In these counter-attack situations, you must move the ball quickly forward before the opponents can get a solid shape behind the ball and block your penetration.

This is the time for a quick long pass and fast running. **When you have them stretched, you must keep them stretched** and work a chance before they can recover.

You may find a central space to attack with the ball early in the counter-attacking move. This will soon be closed by the opponent's available defenders, as they will congregate in the middle to protect the direct route to goal.

Your forwards, looking to get played in from your counter-attacking player, may first need to head for the wings and then make quick angled runs back across the defenders. Take a gamble, play them in and force an opportunity whilst you have the initiative.

The central midfield's unit is every outfield player at different stages of the game. They strive to be available to the full backs, wingers, centre halves and forwards in possession.

Depending on where the ball is on the pitch, they apply pressure with these once the ball is lost. **One of them is always involved in open play** and is always a part of a unit of support for, or pressure on, the man on the ball.

8

Centre Halves

A good team needs a strong spine and a strong spine is strongest at its base. Centre half is not an individual position. **It is a partnership position**.

In a 4-4-2, it is fair to say there are many partnerships, such as the two centre midfielders, the two forwards, and the winger and fullback.

Although these positions do combine their activities, there are many occasions when they are free to pursue a lone trail and work independently of each other.

This is never the case for the centre halves.

They are **two parts of a unit, which can only work correctly in tandem**. Whatever one does must have a direct effect on the position or actions taken up by the other.

Defence is constructed to match the attack it is liable to encounter. In our theoretical local-level standard template, it is the striking pair of the big powerful centre forward, let us say the number 9, and his quicker, more manoeuvrable sidekick, let us say the number 8.

To counteract this, the first contact centre half, the number 5, would be a tall, strong, ball- attacking character. His sidekick, the number 6, would be the speedy, positionally intelligent, sweeper-type individual.

In both centre-half positions, what is desired is experience; or more relevantly a good reader of situations, someone who can sense danger and doesn't hesitate to counter it.

Someone who is proactive, stopping trouble before it starts. This ability comes more frequently in an older player but can be there, naturally, in a good young player.

It can be enough to have one experienced leader in the central partnership who can boss the other into taking up good positions and making timely interventions. Young centre halves learn their trade more quickly if placed alongside a good older colleague.

Indeed, in local soccer, the combination of the old head next to the young legs can work very well as a central unit. The old head still needs decent legs of his own.

The centre halves are the last barrier between the attackers and your goalkeeper, and ultimately your goal. In fact, the goalie could be included in the partnership, such is the close cooperation a good central unit at the back shares with him.

Defending

Centre halves are so close to the goal that what they decide to do can have an immediate effect on the score sheet. Experience is what is most likely to help you make the right decisions and to stop you being caught out of position.

If the forwards miss opportunities, the score line is sadly not affected. If they are out of position, no harm done. If other players make mistakes, in conceding possession or being bypassed, it can still be rectified by the central-defensive partnership.

It is not until these are beaten or absent from their post that you really need to worry.

Centre halves have all the play in front of them. They are perfectly placed to see and read the build up of the opponent's attack. This is why a good central pairing plays a crucial role in leading and directing a team's goal defence. See also chapter 7, *Centre Midfielders*.

They must, however, read the game correctly to command the defence and ensure correct positions are taken up in order to repel the impending attack.

By reading the game correctly, I mean reading the situation as early as possible.

Only then are they able to correctly direct the defensive actions, and organise themselves and their teammates *in time* to nullify any attacking move.

Naive centre halves read danger signs of the game eventually; if you run it on in front of them long enough. By then, the ball may be on the way to your net.

Experience is relative to the standard you are playing at and most local-level centre halves would regularly and instinctively do enough of the right thing and make enough of the right decisions to get by, at their level.

However, when an inexperienced centre half duo meet a gifted individual or a team with superior movement and passing than that which they are used to, they will often find themselves out of position as the move progresses.

For a manager in such games, to heighten their defensive senses, it is worth reminding them of some of the basic defensive tenets that they might not normally apply so strictly.

This chapter is not so concerned with the individual defending technique or common failings of poor centre halves: letting the ball bounce before dealing with it; or backing off too far and leaving it too late to confront an advancing opponent ("he is not my forward, he's a midfielder"); or bad tackling.

It is more about the mindset of what he should be trying to do, in relation to the other parts of a team game, his role in the bigger picture and the reasons for his decisions.

Defenders have two basic defensive lines that they try to hold. They defend the entrance to **the defensive last third**. If this is breached, they fall back and defend **the 18-yard line**.

Each retreat, to the last third and then to the 18-yard box **compacts them centrally** and the defensive incidents become more critical.

If the 18-yard line is ceded, they defend the goal area as far as the goal itself.

They may create a defensive line on the penalty spot or 6-yard box in close situations, as they attempt to give their keeper a space free of attackers and a clear view.

In normal play, with the opponents on the ball still in their own half, they start defending the last third, regrouping there and drawing a line from which they can stage an organised retreat. They do not give up this line easily and they retake it at their first opportunity.

They may be forced to stage a controlled backing off to defend the 18-yard box. From here, they will **close down and challenge opponents**, **intercepting passes and blocking shots**. They do not give up this 18-yard line easily, only when it is breached by man and ball.

Players understand these two lines so it should be possible to instil these starting defensive positions into their play, in such a way that controlling off-sides and a uniform pooling of defensive resources becomes natural and automatic to them.

What you need to avoid is players holding different lines and players dropping off or running towards their own goal, out of harmony with their defensive teammates.

The centre halves should not both be beaten until the ball is on its way into the net, so the area in front of the 18-yard box, and definitely everything in it, is their domain.

Let us consider three relevant premises that arise elsewhere in this book.

The defensive shape evolves as a direct response to the attacking shape and threat used by the opposition. Chapter 1, *Team Shape.*

There are three ways to score in open play, all occur in the last third of the pitch. Chapter 3, *Scoring a Goal.*

The forwards come alive in the last third. Chapter 6, *Strikers.*

If these are true tenets of the game, then the centre halves must also come alive in the last third. They must be very aware of the three ways to score and take up positions and employ strategies to combat the opponent's attempts to set the three ways in motion.

They must adapt these strategies to match the opposition, who may change attacking numbers, personnel or approach during a game.

The *number-5-type centre half* will seek first contact with the target man, *number-9-type centre forward.*

The centre half should try to win any *high balls* up to the centre forward. Due to coming from the blind side of the 9, the 5 should often have the jump on him.

He can judge his jump just a fraction earlier and thereby steal the airspace that the 9 would need to compete for the ball.

For a particularly long or high ball, by dropping off a yard or three he can have a run and jump, as opposed to the 9's backing in or standing jump.

Although the 5 should be favourite for most long high balls, he must not be too eager to win every high ball, as giving away fouls in this area is often worse than allowing the forward to win the header.

This doesn't mean he can't challenge the 9, to stop him having a totally free and therefore possibly more controlled header.

It does mean that **his decision-making has to be good**. A big decision for all defenders is when to fully commit to winning a ball and when to hold off.

The aim is not always to tackle an opponent, but it is always to contain him and force him to use his least dangerous ball-maintenance option.

Stay on your feet; do not get beat, don't foul.

A pass knocked into the forward, below head height, makes the forward the likely winner of that ball. This is definitely *foul territory* for an overly keen centre half.

Only if the 5 has perfectly positioned himself on the 9's shoulder and has read the forward ball should he commit.

Even then, it is dangerous as a clever and brave 9 may suddenly take the space the 5 has seen as his. The 5's commitment then leads to a foul or to being turned by the striker.

Thus, a clever 9 may tempt a 5 into committing for a ball he cannot win by showing a space to the ball that he fully intends later to block.

So the 5 should not get too close to the 9 if a good pass has been laid up to him, especially if the forward has opened his body, sideways on, to receive it. His first touch may be good enough to spin past the 5 or away from him, opening up space behind.

Conversely, a clever 5 can tempt a 9 into taking up the wrong angle to a ball, hesitating or controlling it, into the 5's path.

The 5 should always let the 9 know he is there, by bumping up against him and shouting his team instructions from just behind. By a small contact, low down one side of the 9 as the ball is played up, and then challenging around the other side, he may make the 9 turn into him with the ball instead of away.

Let the 9 know you are there and close, but **keep him guessing as to your exact location**. Contact on the 9 and then back off just as he receives the ball. **Being too close is a big problem**, as he may quickly spin on a good or fortunate first touch.

For dealing with one-on-ones, that is, an attempted run past him with the ball, a defender should realise that being in the way is not the same as moving into the way. It is not obstruction.

A central defender can and should be a big object to go around.

He should read the forward's intended path and turn into that space, whilst heading after the ball as soon as it is played and before the forward can claim that space as his own.

The forwards will try and stretch the play. This will make it easier for balls to be played up to them and into space, from the back. **You must not let them dictate the line**.

I am generally **not keen on playing offside** or keeping what might be considered **a high line** at any stage of the opposition's ball possession.

A high line, especially one without an effective squeeze on the ball, encourages and will be undone by a measured midfield pass in behind the central pairing for a quick forward to run on to. Late runs and dribbles from midfield will also find it out.

I believe the offside line should occur naturally and rarely be forced; forced, such as at opposition free kicks.

As an opposition move develops, the central pairing should hold their first defensive line around the entrance to their last third.

The centre forwards will be trying to push them deeper before it is necessary, and this must be resisted.

The position of the player on the ball dictates the offside line, not the forwards.

The line is never rigid but constantly self-adjusting.

Using the offside trap as a deliberate ploy, by committing at all costs to holding this line and even pushing further out just before the opposition play a forward pass is a high-risk policy.

I recommend side/back-pedalling just before the ball is played and dealing with it by actual, physical defending. Rely first on yourselves not on the referee's assistant.

If a striker is making naive mistimed forward runs that are clearly too far ahead of the play, then you have to, as a back four, hold your line and let him go.

This should happen naturally and you *must not be* naïve enough to cover such a run.

If you cover the obvious offside run, you cause the pitch to stretch into your danger area and you give the opposition a free trip into it. **Defence without an initial holding line will be difficult**.

The fullbacks take their line from the centre halves, but the 5 and the 6 should always keep an eye to ensure that their fullbacks are not dropping deeper than themselves.

It can be a big problem if they decide to let a forward run offside, only to find a fullback keeping him on.

If the centre halves are letting a mistimed forward runner move unmarked into offside, they should **check first that they are the last man**.

Whilst holding the defensive last third line, **the boss centre half may regularly raise his arms** to briefly form a cross.

His defence colleagues should always take this as a sign to align their positions.

The centre half should, by looking quickly along the line of his arms, see that his fullbacks and central colleague are not behind him and the offside run if it comes is safe to let go.

A split second before the forward pass is made, they must stop or slow their covering action to **make the offside more obvious**. They should raise their arms as the pass is made and appeal for offside.

This doesn't mean they stop playing. Not until the whistle is blown.

The forward pass may not go to the player in the offside position or he may totally ignore it and be deemed "not interfering"; in which case, play continues and they should be ready to back off or chase anyone coming from an onside position.

A natural synchronised backing-off towards your goal by the central two, as the move progresses, is the norm. If the opposition's move breaks down in this early phase, then the centre halves, having dropped off, should **quickly retake the last third line**.

The 5 must, during the opposition lead up play into his defensive last third, mark the 9 closely. Win what is clearly winnable; otherwise contain the situation, including conceding the first phase to the attackers if the attack builds into your last third.

Defending the second phase of the attack inside your last third may involve dropping deeper around the edge of your 18-yard box.

Now you are **worried about the three ways to score**.

Whilst the 5 is marking the target man 9, the sweeper-type 6 is marking the more free running number-8-type centre forward.

The movement of the opponent striker 8 dictates the movement of the centre half 6. He **keeps goal-side**; **passing him on** when the number 8's movement threatens to drag the 6 too far out of position.

First and foremost, **they are defending the goal, not babysitting the forwards**.

A lot of runs are designed to lure you out of position. Let a striker pick the ball up on the wing, rather than leave a gap in the middle for another opponent to run through.

The centre halves should never get too close to each other in this phase. Although they are **both man-marking**, they are also **zonally defending the routes to goal**.

They do not want to be so close that the same forward's spin or move beats them both.

They do not want to be in a position where they can both be tempted to go for the same ball.

First contact should be made by one centre half as the other quickly drops off, on the cover.

At this point, the centre halves will need to bring at least one of the fullbacks in to help cover any steep attacking passes. Your winger should now be looking after that fullback's area.

At this stage of the opposition's attack, all hands are on deck trying to plug the gaps that might lead to an attempt on goal, via the three ways to score in open play.

Anywhere within and around the 18-yard box is the red alert danger area for the defenders.

The two defensive lines of four are almost on top of each other as all are working to deny a cross, shot, steep pass or dribble through.

They cannot stand off too far, but must put pressure on all opposition movement and the man in possession, being careful not to foul.

As soon as the ball is cleared or possession is won, both lines of four should move quickly up the pitch to regain some territory and force the opposition out of the danger area.

Both forwards may make runs out to the wings. At no point should both centre halves leave their central-defending position at the same time.

A lot of the forward's movement attempts to drag the centre halves out of the central position. It is okay for one centre half to cover this move, but the other now has to remain central and bring the free full back in a bit closer.

At our level, we often see both centre halves out with their full backs allowing an opposition midfielder, who essentially becomes a centre forward, to attack the central space.

The centre halves must learn to pass their player on. If the centre forward goes out to the wing or drops deep into midfield, he is *no longer a centre forward*.

In this case, and especially if your fellow centre half is already out of position, you must pass him on to your full back or midfield — even if the forward is now running around loose, unmarked, in central midfield or on the wing.

He can't score from out there but if you go out and join him, leaving the centre unguarded, one of his teammates making a late run through the middle might.

You can always pick him up when he returns to the central area, so keep an eye on him.

I liken it sometimes to zombies attacking your house! Your wife and child are inside and you repel the attack; and then you decide to go chasing them down the street and leave the house unguarded. Never forget what you are meant to be guarding: the goal.

It doesn't really matter what goes on out on the wing or how outnumbered you may be in midfield. Not enough, that you both might desert the central defensive position to fix it.

Essentially because they cannot score from there.

What does matter is, are the opponents, whatever the number on their backs might say, marked in and around the box where they can score?

Central defenders have to **focus on defending the goal**. If they have to cede possession by refusing to desert this mission, then so be it. **Winning the ball is not the prime object**, **preventing goals is**.

As soon as the attacking team are in the last third and preparing to attempt one of the three ways to score, the centre halves should both be exactly that, centre halves, and not full backs or midfielders.

If the move has reached its third phase into the 18-yard box, then both centre halves must at this point be central. There should be no big spaces between them.

With their central midfielders they are a **human wall**, blocking the goal from 20-yard shots. They must be brave and make themselves large, as the ball can slip through the smallest of gaps.

The two centre halves are also there to **attack and cover** any ball passed into the 18-yard box and so must make sure that their central midfielders are closing down any opposition and the possibility of a pass, dribble or shot from around and outside of the box.

Avoid unnecessary challenges in the 18-yard box. The object is always to prevent a goal; not to tackle the opponent. **Stay on your feet; don't get beat**. Avoidable penalties break a manager's heart.

They should be **touch tight in the box**.

This means you can reach out arm's length and touch the striker. Be goal-side on his shoulder. Try to be **where you can see him better than he can see you**.

If you are turned around and forced to run into your own box, then **mark the opposition**. You will be surprised how often they will attract the ball.

Try not to ball watch. Ball watching is the enemy of good defending.

When the opposition winger is running down the flank, deep into your last third and threatening a cross, you should not be watching him, at least not with both eyes.

You should have your good eye on the runs from his fellow forwards.

Before the cross, have a quick look around at the threats in the box. **The ball will not go into the goal by itself**. One of these people you are looking at will have got to it beforehand. Make sure they are touch-tight marked, at arm's length and goal-side.

Defenders must **expect the worst in the 18-yard box**. They must expect a perfect cross delivered onto the centre forward's instep or forehead.

They cannot set up their positions *as if they were the target* for the cross. They can *only* mark space if they have the numbers spare to do so or if that space is inevitably where the cross must arrive. That is the decision-making dilemma of a centre half in the box.

Sometimes if the crosser/winger is closed down and has only one area to put the ball into, it is okay for the centre half to take up a position cutting off this entry angle at its nearest point. He has chosen to cut off the supply because the supply could only come in one way.

The trouble with this is choosing to do it and not marking the attackers in the box when the winger has more than one available area to put his cross. If the winger is not closed down enough, he can lift his cross over the centre half or pull it back behind him.

In this case, the centre half is left stranded marking space, vainly trying to cut off the supply when he should have been marking an opponent attacking his goal.

An unexpectedly good cross from a difficult position will always find you out if you are marking space. The natural defender will probably choose to mark the goal threat, whilst the sweeper-type wants to cut off the supply.

This can work on a team basis and many crosses will be dealt with by such a system, until that unexpectedly good cross comes in. Marking in the box is hard to fault and when marking space leaves men unmarked to score, it looks terrible for the defence.

The defender is not a forward looking for the most likely point of supply. He is a centre half looking for the forward who is looking for the most likely point of supply. He is a goal defender looking to mark the most likely goal-scoring threat in their box.

He must **fear the worst and mark his man**, regardless of the seemingly innocuous position he may have temporarily taken up.

If the cross avoids them both, then all is well and good. At least that forward was marked and was never going to get onto it. **Space doesn't score, unmarked forwards do**.

The man to mark in the box may change.

You should make sure the **players nearest the goal are marked first**, even if you have to let your man's run go, in order to pick one up in a more dangerous position.

Passing players on, delegation and communication are the skills required here.

The goal area is not a quiet place. The centre halves and the goalkeeper should be constantly providing defensive advice and informing each other of goal threats. There is no excuse for attackers sneaking in unseen.

It is better that the centre halves deal with a cross or an attempt at one-on-one, if possible. **The goalkeeper is and should be the last defence**. If he seems unsure, let him know when he should come and when he should stay.

The goalkeeper and the centre halves have to work together on this crucial communication of who is to deal with which problem.

It may be frantic and desperate communication. It may seem often confused and contradictory to the inexperienced ear, but it is necessary if the right decisions for the team are to be made. See chapter 5, *Goalkeepers*.

A defender's header or clearance is up in the air and far away, not down. This is to give your players a chance to put pressure on that ball before it lands. Downward headers and low clearances are only for a definite pass to your own man.

Strikers can be lazy at getting out of the box when the ball is partially cleared and can present you with an easy, pressure-releasing offside opportunity.

If you decide to keep them on, they may get an easy opportunity to score against you.

You should be clear as a team that if the ball leaves the 18-yard box, all players must follow it out and try to reach at least the penalty spot area *before* it might be returned; whilst **keeping an eye for onside attackers moving the other way**.

A good centre half should always be ushering his team up and out whenever the ball is partially cleared or held up, creating a new defensive line that little bit further from the goal, where the keeper has more of a chance to save a direct shot.

Clearances should be calm and definitive, not panicky and desperate.

Definitive in that the ball is dealt with, ending that particular move; cleared out of the last third, up front or out of play, where the defence can push out and reposition themselves.

Panic and desperation are not choices you need to make — when the right time for that comes it is probably too late.

Attacking

Attack is the best form of defence. The defensive line provides the ideal space to bring the ball under good possession, i.e. head up, facing the opposition and with time to pick a pass.

I have detailed in the pass-and-move chapter how **the back curved line in possession is the ideal place to start the pass-and-move game,** in that the players have a large space to operate in and they outnumber their opponents in that space.

If the back line is comfortable on the ball, they will provide safe out passes for their midfield and will leave them space in which to play.

The centre halves should not be marking their forwards when their midfielders have possession. As described in the *Team Shape* chapter, they should not be squeezing play when they are in possession, but expanding to provide safe out passes.

The centre halves should be happy to be on the ball around the edge of their box when there are only two forwards trying to pressure them. Their central position allows them to choose which direction play should go, out to the wings or through the middle.

They should be happy to be 10-35 yards apart or whatever distance is necessary to create a safe angle or an unthreatened position for each other, in order to maintain possession.

A good defensive line, led by at least one good ball-playing centre half, should be able to carry the ball up to the halfway line from the edge of their box, simply by playing the ball to- and-fro along this line, with occasional help from the midfield and goalkeeper.

When they have reached the halfway line, they should still **drop to provide a safe out** and switch of wings if necessary.

This means they should quickly be able to **switch play from one full back or winger to the wide players on the other side of the pitch**, by going safely around the back. This is sometimes called "around the houses" in soccer jargon.

Squeezing back onto their forwards after the breakdown of ball possession is part of providing the curved line and safe out-ball style of play. It should always be in their minds that as soon as this ball is turned over, they need to mark their nearest central threat.

Expand and contract is the central defender's game. When to play soccer and when to clear the ball are the big decisions that can only be made by the centre halves. Obviously, it is better to be safe than sorry. *When in doubt, kick it out.*

The centre halves and defensive midfielder must be thinking of a possible turnover of the ball when the rest are attacking the opponent's last third. Only then will they be ready to manage the transition and snuff out the counter attack.

They must **concentrate at all times**. Good defensive players expect the worst.

The goalkeeper should be a safe out for the centre halves. If you want him to clear the ball play it back along the ground, away from the goal, to his preferred side, at a temperature he can deal with.

If you want him to maintain early possession and start a move in your own last third, then play it to his feet like a normal pass-and-move, giving him a safe return-pass angle. See the *Pass and Move* chapter for starting possession from the goalkeeper.

A good clearance from the back is often up to the corner flags, which can turn the opposition around and even lead to your own team's possession high up the pitch.

The **occasional foray into midfield**, if a good opportunity presents itself, **can tip the balance of power** providing easier penetration into the attacking last third.

Going up for corners and staying there for the second phase of a corner or follow-on attack would usually be the extent of a centre half's direct intervention in attacking play.

A good attacker of a ball might also go up front for the last five minutes or so, if the present state of play dictates.

The main focus for the centre halves has to be containment of the opponent's attack and defence of the goal. Composure on the ball and a willingness to start and sustain the pass- and-move game is a means to the same end.

The centre-halves' unit will involve their keeper, full backs and central midfielders.

9

Full Backs

In my 35-year experience of adult soccer, full backs have changed their general characteristics. In 1980, your typical decent non-league full back would have been a tough tackling, fast, sturdy, pit bull of a character.

He would have been totally focused on stopping his winger and helping his centre halves.

Nowadays, they tend to be accomplished ball carriers, and are **expected to provide width and penetration**, particularly in the early phases of possession.

The ideal full back is quick and has a cool, composed manner on the ball. He is equally able to pass a long ball up to the forwards as a shorter ball inside to his midfielders. He is comfortable in possession and consistently available.

The full back hugging the touchline is fundamental to the required shape in possession that enables a pass-and-move game.

In the arched shape in possession, the full back would be mostly unmarked in his own half. Therefore, it is vital that he is happy to be on the ball, otherwise the first phase of possession play will not be possible.

The defenders in possession would normally outnumber their opposition forwards four to two. The two full-back positions are most likely to offer a "safe out" pass and enable build up of possession because they are the positions on the pitch most likely to be unmarked.

When the defenders create the arched shape over the full width of the pitch, they should be able to retain possession of the ball long enough to approach the halfway line.

If, for example, the right full back is under pressure and has no easy forward pass, he should be able to look over his left shoulder and see one of his centre halves.

Equally, the left back, if in possession, should always be able to look over his right shoulder and see the other centre half in the arched defensive line 15-25 yards away.

If this centre half is unmarked, the full back can routinely play the ball to him and, retaining good possession, the centre half can continue the move.

At this stage, leaving their own last defensive third area, with their head up and the ball under control, they should be able to play it accurately up and into their own forwards or midfielders.

The bread-and-butter pass for a full back in his wide position should be into the hub of the team, i.e. into his central midfielders or back to his centre half for a switch of direction.

Defending

The full back's direct defending task is to look after the opposition winger and, indeed, any opposition attacks into their own last third area.

By **marking the winger tight**, the full back can deter the wingers' teammates from passing to him in the first place. Thus, if he does receive the ball, it is often with his back to the full back.

If the winger is markedly quicker than the full back, it may be necessary to stand a couple of paces off him. This may mean the winger can receive the ball facing the full back, but it should give the full back enough of an advantage, if balls are played in behind him, to counter the winger's pace.

This again is one of those soccer decisions that can only be made on the pitch, by the player himself. Soccer theory is a guide and decision-making about which part of the theory to ignore or employ will always be key.

If the winger, with the ball at his feet, gets a run at the full back, the full back must be quite clear in his mind what, as full back, he should be trying to do.

The object is not necessarily to tackle the winger, but is primarily to **stop the winger doing what he wants to do**. The winger wants to go past the full back and either head for goal or put a dangerous cross or pass into the box.

It is the **full back's job to prevent crosses** or at least prevent dangerous ones.

If the full back is trying too hard to tackle the winger, he *may get beaten* by committing himself to a tackle he cannot win. He may *give a free kick away*. Both of these defeat the object.

He should get in the winger's face, that is, get within a couple of paces so that any loose touch by the winger can be intercepted.

This will also deter the winger from crossing the ball, as the full back, if close, is likely to block it. If the winger does cross the ball, the nearer the full back is to him, the harder an accurate or decently shaped cross becomes.

He should set himself at an angle to the winger, so that he can **force the winger either inside or down the line**. He should never get square-on, unless making a tackle or getting beaten.

Higher up the pitch, it may make sense for the full back to **force the winger inside**.

Nearer his own goal, it would be better to **force him wide** so that he cannot strike at goal.

A full back who sets himself in this way also delays the winger. Jumping in to a tackle or standing too far off a winger will encourage the winger to attack the space or put in a decent cross. Being close, and at an angle, delays and restricts the winger's options. The winger may have to attempt a dribble or a safe out pass.

By **jockeying and delaying the winger**, the full back buys time for his defensive teammates. They will have time to mark the opposition forwards and prepare for any cross or run from the winger.

Stay on your feet; do not get beat, don't foul.

A *second defender* will also have time to move into support for him so that the full back knows that if he is forced or tempted to tackle, he has back-up.

If the winger attempts to push the ball and run using his pace, the full back should immediately turn and sprint after the ball, while taking the winger's direct route to it.

This, if done early enough using his two-yards positional advantage, will not be deemed obstruction; but will **ensure the winger has to bend his run around the defender** and produces a more equal race.

If the race is lost, the full back should now direct his own run on a shorter path to the goal. A central defender may move across and help him out. It is now time for the full back to mark another opponent running into the box or try to head the winger off later in his run.

These are all common-sense things to do that are regularly forgotten by full backs in the heat of battle.

The crucial and often bitter nature of the contest between a winger and a full back often leads to some brain switch-off by a rattled full back, and even obvious defensive basics are ignored.

The full back may concentrate too much on the winger and forget that he is actually defending a threat to his area and ultimately the goal, and not a specific player.

When the winger is not on the wing, he is not a winger.

If he moves central, he should be passed on, to be the responsibility of the more central defenders and midfielders. Remember that just because the opposition lose their shape, you do not have to.

Passing people on, when they are carrying the ball or making a run across the pitch, saves the legs of your team by sharing the task whilst depleting the individual opponent's energy.

By this timed sharing and swapping of tasks, you can maintain a presence when and where it is needed.

If they swamp the midfield area, you should be able to rely on your strong team spine to cope with a larger number of opponents in a confined central area; happy in the knowledge that when you have the ball, the rewards for you on the wings should compensate for any difficulty with possession in the middle.

Good possession on the wings is often better, because it provides the opportunity to deliver the best of the three ways to score in open play and is much safer in case of a turnover than possession in the middle.

If the ball is in his half, but on the other wing, and the shape has compacted on that side, the full back should sit in nearer to the centre half.

He should **never position himself further over than the centre of the field**. If he does so, an opponent *will sneak* into his vacant area.

He should have an eye on the switch pass that could bring the ball very quickly onto his wing and he should be cover for a ball in behind his centre half on his side of the pitch.

He should be aware of the possibility that he may keep a player, making a run that he cannot cover, onside; so, as a rule, he should not be nearer his own goal line than the central defenders.

In particular, he should be careful not to keep his winger's run onside if the central defenders choose to hold their line. **The full back always takes his defensive offside line from his centre halves**.

It is better that a deep-laying centre half might keep his winger onside than that the full back might inadvertently, while covering his winger's movement, keep a central forward onside.

The full back is further forward in the curved back line in ball possession. The line becomes flat in defensive mode, as the centre halves push onto the centre forwards. The full back can drop only so far as the centre halves' chosen line.

At this stage, it is for the centre halves to side/back-pedal first and set a new defensive line as the ball looks to be played forward.

The full back should never decide to drop deeper first and keep a run onside. The risk is that he could keep a centre forward onside by covering a winger's run — a winger's run which is then not the object of the forward pass.

He has to keep one eye on his winger and one eye on his centre halves' defensive line. The positioning of the **full back's body angle**, **slightly open to view infield**, should help this.

The non-interfering rule makes offside an acute problem for present-day full backs.

A player's **decision-making determines a good player** from a bad one.

When the ball threatens to be crossed into your box from the *opposite* wing, the full back should take up a position guarding the far post. He should make sure that a deep cross that passes his centre halves is not met by an opposition wide player attacking that far post.

Marking in the box needs to be goal-side and touch-tight. All defenders should be able to reach out a hand and touch the person they are marking.

When the perfect cross comes in, you will have no chance to put the attacker off his strike unless you can physically challenge him. Ball-watching leads to marking space, not opponents. Space doesn't score, people do.

Attacking

The full back should support his winger. He should not get too close to his winger. 5-20 yards behind him would usually be perfect support.

He should not overlap and pass the winger out, *unless* the winger has opened his body angle or is facing the opposition's goal and has the ball under control; or *unless the full back is certain* of being on the end of a midfielder's pass down the line, as in a "**third man running**" situation.

You often see a winger receiving a ball in the opposition's half, whilst marked, *with his back to the opposition goal* and the full back will go flying past him up the line. This is only good if the winger can pass the ball back to a midfielder, who can then play it quickly to the full back steaming up the line, as the third man in the move.

Invariably though, the winger, now with no full back supporting and no safe inside pass to a midfielder, risks losing the ball and providing the opposition with a chance to break up a wing, now missing its full back.

Therefore, a full back flying past a winger *facing the wrong way* in local soccer is usually a big mistake. Only when the full back is sure the winger has a wall pass for him or another safe, supporting pass to a central midfielder, should he try it.

It is great for a team's creative play when a winger and a full back have a good two-versus- one move in their locker, which usually involves a wall pass or the central midfielder to set up.

The full back, if he can get up a head of steam, can play a one-two with his winger that will lose his marker, with the winger at the same time taking the opponent's full back out of his full back position.

The winger must make a timed move inside, opening an angle to receive the pass and opening his body to return the pass, whilst tempting the opposition full back to follow him.

The full back then plays the ball into his own winger and flies past his marker (the opposition winger), as the latter often ball-watches the wall pass.

The full back has now swapped jobs with his own winger and chases the ball into the space vacated by the opposing full back; a typical full back-winger combined attacking move.

In choosing to support the winger 5-20 yards further back down the line, he provides a safe out to his winger. If the winger is not happy taking his opposition full back on or crossing the ball himself, he can always turn around safe in the knowledge that his full back is instructed to be behind; supporting him.

Chipped and longish balls into the centre forward are also a constant way out for a full back. He should keep an eye out for the sudden dart forward and offer that a good number-9-type forward will be doing.

These passes should preferably be below head height, so that the number 9 can do more with it. High, long balls give the centre half a chance, often making him favourite.

If the full back manages to get into the opposition's last third of the pitch, the decisions become easier. **In the last third of the pitch, everyone on the attacking team should be thinking of the three ways to score**.

The most likely way for the full back to get involved is with a cross from the wings into the attacking last third of the pitch, with the forwards or midfielders attacking the ball as it arrives into the area. See chapter 3, *Scoring a Goal*.

If the full back chooses to put a ball into the box from a wide last third area, it is up to the forwards and midfielders to make sure they have a presence in there.

In local-level soccer, I would always **encourage the full backs in possession of the ball in the attacking last third to cross the ball**, i.e. put the ball in the box.

Why risk losing possession with an extra pass to the winger if it is a difficult pass or if the winger is not in a much better position to cross than the full back?

If you have full backs that do not hesitate to cross a ball in the attacking last third, then the next step is to make sure the forwards and attacking midfielders are willing to make runs into the box. **First, make sure that crosses are plentiful**; forward runs to get into the box will naturally follow.

When I see a full back cross the ball from a last third position into an opposition box that is devoid of any of our attacking players, I would be more likely to encourage (shout at) our attacking players than to criticise the full back for crossing into an empty box.

If the midfielders and forwards are confident that a ball will be delivered regularly into the box when the full back is in possession in the last third, they will be willing to make runs into the opponent's box.

If the cross cannot pick out an attacker, it should be bent in at a reasonable pace behind the defence, enticing the goalkeeper to come for it and your own forwards to attack it.

The attacking full back on the other side of the pitch should be on the edge of the opposition's last third, available to pick up any clearance from the defenders or to pressure the ball if the cross is long.

He is also acting as cover, giving depth in the full-back position should the attacking run or cross of the other full back be turned into a counter-attack situation.

Indeed, both full backs should be prepared, on a successful defence of the cross, for a possible 60-yard run back towards their own goal in response to any counter-attack.

Full backs should have the aerobic capacity to cover the area from deep in the attacking last third to their own penalty box, throughout a 90-minute game, occasionally at full pace.

A late, discreet and decisive **blindside attacking run by an overlapping full back**, around and behind an opposing team watching the action on the other side of the pitch, will only be made by a strong runner.

Obviously, this is a bit of a tall order for a local-level team full back. Nevertheless, the **full backs should be amongst the fittest members of the team** and its most able distance runners…at least one of them should be…whilst the other could be the more conservative and solid defensive type.

Their game is always about contracting onto the opposition when they have the ball, and expanding off them when you have it.

This is very important for full backs because they need to be available in all phases of possession, yet they need to closely guard their winger and provide cover for the centre halves.

The full back and winger are another of a team's paired units and must work in unison. The full back and the winger's roles are often interchangeable.

They need to understand both roles, in order to bring the best out of their individual games and dovetail into each other's tasks.

10

Wingers

Good wing play is the natural embodiment of all that is beautiful in the game of soccer. Wingers are often fast, skilful dribblers, who do not hesitate to attack opponent defenders and drive into the attacking last third.

Spectators focus when a winger gets the ball and sets himself to take on the full back.

At this stage in a game, the attacking team has already done well to get the ball out to the winger in the opponent's half and facing his full back.

They are now very close to creating **the most productive of the three ways to score in open play**; **a cross**. Even better if it is crossed after stranding a full back and making the by-line. No wonder the winger grabs our attention.

Many youngsters hold the position of winger. Pace, a willingness to run and a certain unpredictability are assets that most suit wing play. It is a great position to learn an all-round game from, as **it encompasses attack**, **midfield and defence**.

It is also a position where a *learner* cannot disrupt a team too badly in the event that he does not do the job properly.

A winger of the David Beckham mode can be more effective than a pacy dribbler. This type of winger uses his soccer brain and passing/

crossing ability as an alternative to pace and dribbling skills. Pace and dribbling can be unpredictable in their outcome and **a clever winger is generally more consistently productive**.

This chapter is about how a winger should set about his task, again in theoretical terms on a percentage basis. If you do the routine and obvious things most of the time, you will get better results overall than if you consistently try the difficult things.

You cannot teach speed and largely you cannot teach the ability to beat an opponent. You can train at these, but the results of a natural physical ability combined with years of dribbling practice as a youngster will always outshine anything learned by an adult in training sessions.

This is especially so when training sessions are held just twice a week, as is the case with most local soccer clubs.

What you can teach is positioning and an understanding of what is the winger's role and best option in most circumstances. The winger needs to understand what he should be trying to do in his various roles, at various stages during the game.

Most importantly, you can **teach a winger how to get the ball**. Many fast, dribbling wingers are marked out of a game too easily because they do not pay enough attention to the skill of receiving the ball, and making and keeping themselves available.

Defending

Defensively, **the winger has to protect his full back**, not only from the opposing full back but also on occasion from the opposing winger.

The winger and his full back are each other's second defender, giving cover and security, so that one might fully commit to confronting the opponent on the ball.

In the modern game, the full back is an often-used attacking force. They will break quickly up the line as soon as they sense their opposition winger has left them unattended.

The winger has to track back and oppose the full back, limiting the kind of forward passes and runs available to him.

It can be a policy for a winger to let the opposing full back go, in the defensive last third. In a good team, set up for counter-attack, he can rely on the defensive midfielders and defence to win the ball whilst he saves his legs and lungs.

When the ball is turned over, he is fresh and ready to punish the opposing full back for his trip up front. This is a calculated risk often worth taking.

When to track back and when to stay up and pass the full back on to others is one of those decisions that determines whether you are a good player or not.

Good players make good decisions most of the time and sticking to your defensive task, or taking a calculated risk and staying in space, is a big decision for a winger.

It can depend on the state of play or just on the feeling a winger has, that this time he can afford to let the full back go, that the defence can deal with it.

As a manager, you can insist that the winger never lets the opposing full back run free. In this case, you will be missing a winger many times when the ball breaks in your favour.

For me, it is best to leave these decisions to the natural instinct of the winger and to the defensive leaders on the pitch. If they want him all the way back, they will let him know.

When the opposition are attacking on the opposite side of the pitch and especially entering the defensive third, *he will need to track back* and fill in for the full back.

This is because his full back will have tucked in to the centre to help his centre halves or to cover for a centre half out of position.

The winger needs to act like a full back in this position, employing safety first, watching his offside line, delaying opponents, forcing them away from goal and preventing crosses.

A winger has a large area from goal line to goal line to cover. He must be aerobically fit if he is going to do this effectively. He must be adept at passing opponents on (communicating) when they leave his area and marking new ones who occasionally stray into it.

If he follows players out of his area, he is compromising the shape of the team and he is putting pressure on a teammate's position. **He must squeeze and mark in his area** and pass on opponents who move from it.

The winger's area is from end to end, and between the 18-yard box and the throw line. He should generally only be further in if he is actually on the ball or inside each 18-yard box.

He should develop an understanding with his full back because the two positions are interchangeable and certainly work best in conjunction with, not separate from, each other.

Winger and full back are so similar that often an aggressive winger will make a great full back, and a skilful full back a great winger.

Winger and full back are another of a team's paired units and must work in unison. See chapter 9, *Full backs*.

Attacking

In the build-up play, **the winger should hug his touchline** and constantly adjust his angle to his teammates so as to be available as an out pass.

The winger should really come alive in the attacking last third and until then be happy to help win, maintain and recycle possession.

Many local-league wingers are great when they get the ball in the right position, but really bad at getting possession in the first place.

This has as much to do with the starting position they take up as the movement they employ from it.

The winger should hug the touchline when his team has possession. A good winger plays side-on to the game, ready to receive the ball with an open body. Even if the ball is on the other wing, he should never be more than 20-25 yards from his line.

This is because if a switch of play is going to be possible, he has to be in position, ready.

He will never be able to move quicker than the ball and if he has to chase it out to the wing from a central position, the opposition will also have time to move over and the point of the switch is gone. See chapter 1, *Team Shape*.

The point of the switch is to catch the opposition out, to catch them squeezing too much on one side of the pitch — a very common occurrence in local soccer.

By quickly switching the ball either through your team shape with a couple of passes or with one long pass, inroads can be easily made into the opposition's last third.

Width *is a vital function* that the winger provides to other members of the team.

Width stretches the pitch and creates gaps between the central defenders that can be exploited by a midfielder or the second striker, driving through.

By staying wide, a winger can provide a safe out pass to his teammates, which in certain situations protects them from losing the ball.

He does not squeeze his own central midfield players. Instead, he gives them room to play.

The angles and distances created if he stays wide become so large that the opposition find it difficult to pressure the ball, especially given local-level fitness standards.

When I say the winger must stay wide, in a pure footballing sense I mean somebody should be in this position. It does not have to always be the winger. If the winger swaps with the forward or his width is temporarily provided by the full back, then all is well and good.

In fact, swapping runs across each other is a part of good movement.

At local-league level, we should walk before we can run. You can ask the winger to play *total football* or you can get him to generally stay wide.

Staying wide is not the only requisite for receiving the ball and providing a safe out pass.

The winger must keep *opening the angles* between himself and his teammates on the ball.

He does this by moving off his starting position, say between 5 to 25 yards up and down the line, and from 20 yards in-field to the touchline and back; *constant back, forth, across, zigzag- type movement* designed to lose his marker, if only by a few yards.

This, **timed to suit the man on the ball**, would ensure that the winger receives his fair share of passes. This movement is also perfect for the one-two, wall-pass moves which may help set a midfielder, striker or his full back in behind a defensive line.

I often see a local winger apparently marking the opposition full back, though the winger's team are in good possession. I am sure the winger will think it is him that is being marked but I know that **a good winger would not be standing** there, **marked by the full back**.

The winger can drop a bit deeper to pick up the ball. The opposition full back cannot just go and mark the winger, no matter how deep he drops. The full back always has to worry about the bigger picture, i.e. protecting his centre halves and the goal.

Therefore, the winger should always be able to find space to receive the ball around the halfway line area by dropping a little deeper.

Further up the pitch the full back will be able to mark him close, so a little in-and-out movement is necessary if the winger is to attract the ball or create space for others.

Going short to get the ball long is one move a good winger employs.

He can move toward his full back who is on the ball, bringing his marker with him. The full back ignores his short offer and instead chips it past the winger and on up to the late short run of a centre forward. The winger instantly spins as the ball passes him and attacks the free space down the line. The forward now tries to feed him in.

Going long to get the ball short is where the winger, after bringing his full back short, spins and drives the full back long as if looking for a ball over the top. He then applies the brakes and turns, going back to receive the ball short. It's all in the timing. You won't always get it right.

The in-and-out and up-and-down movement of a winger is non-stop, and sometimes subtle and unproductive, so the local-league winger may consider it a waste of time and energy.

Good movement is a fundamental difference between a winger playing a decent standard and a lower-level one. It is **the difference between having the ball and not having it**.

If you only make a move when you have a definite chance to receive the ball, you are predictable. That is not a good thing for a player in a forward position to be. It is also a selfish way to play and does the rest of the team no creative favours.

The winger should time and direct his runs to match the build-up play of his playmaker and centre forwards. A sudden burst into the space left by a departing forward may attract the ball. A timed position-swap with a forward at pace may be enough for one of them to end up on the ball. Being static is not an option.

You must time your runs to complement the striker's movement.

When a striker makes a run further up the pitch into your wing space, you should make a run into his forward channel. This helps the striker's move by keeping the opposition centre half busy covering your run.

It also provides a forward around the box if your striker gets in a cross from your wing. You do him and your team no service if you insist on staying on your wing too.

It is a difficult skill for a winger, used to travelling at speed with the ball, watching his own feet as he dribbles, to get his head up and pick out a pass at the opportune moment.

It is often easier for slower moving, upright midfielders to pick a pass. I believe wingers are sometimes overly criticised for lack of vision. You may as well criticise the head-up, holding midfielder for not being able to put his head down and beat a man.

Really **good wingers can get their heads up and pick out a forward with their crosses** and it is a quality your average speedy winger needs to work on.

I would be happy if one winger had the ability to go head-down past his full back and then hammer in a cross, and the other was the more cerebral pass-and-move-type.

Another lesson for wingers to learn is that after a burst down the wing, **the space is always behind them**. This means that the damage they have done by thrusting 20 yards into the last third is not in front of them, but behind them.

In front of them, the opposition is closing in, closing down the space. If he keeps on going or plays the ball forward, there is a big chance of losing possession. If he checks his run and turns around, he can survey the damage he has inflicted on the opposition.

He will see his midfield colleagues and his full back running up to fill the new space he has created for the team. He will see the opposition midfield running towards its own goal, trying to set up a new, deeper, defensive line.

If he now maintains possession by passing back or square into the new space claimed by him and his team, he has taken advantage of his good run and not squandered it.

The move can continue now with the three ways to score in everybody's head, as they hit the attacking last third of the pitch.

In the attacking last third the winger may scorn a narrow window to cross because he knows 20 yards behind him in support will be the full back, with more time to get his head up and pick a player with his cross.

If he scorns the chance to cross, looks back and sees that the full back is not 20 yards behind him but 40 yards away, still marking his winger: welcome to lower local-league level.

I played a match on the wing as a young man and my central midfielder was Martin Peters, a World Cup winner, who at the end of his career was playing non-league.

He passed to me regularly around the centre of the pitch and I would hare off down the line to attack the full back.

Martin would shout at me to stop and pass the ball back to him, which I did, and he would then often progress the move in another direction.

After a good few of these runs, where I had to check and pass the ball back to him as he followed me up the pitch, I was getting a bit frustrated. I wanted to keep going and get past the full back and not stop every time I had made a few yards.

Eventually, I ended up shouting back at him that he just wanted me to do his running, to stop ordering me about, and to let me get on with my own game.

I hardly had a kick after that, as the passes from Martin Peters dried up.

It took me a few years to learn the lesson from that. I eventually realised that a winger is mainly there to make inroads into the opposition's space by skilful darting runs that stretch the game and consolidate the team's territorial claim.

He provides penetration. The vast majority of times he has to check and pass back into the space he has created, so that the whole team can move up the pitch and more teammates can get into the attacking last third.

The more teammates in the attacking last third, the more chances of creating a decent opportunity from one of the three ways to score.

It is not a go-for-bust situation each time and by taking advantage of the space he has made he may receive the ball again during the move, even deeper in the last third, where this time he can try the decisive run and cross that he so wants to do.

A winger beating his full back creates space as another of the opposing team is forced to confront him, potentially freeing-up another area of the pitch that can be exploited.

The winger should not show the full back his tricks for free, by beating him or teasing him on the halfway line when a pass would have been adequate. He should make the full back pay to see them, punishing him with them, as he goes by him, into the last third.

If the ball is out wide, the game has an ability to be stretched, forcing opposition central defenders wide, creating space for runs through and crosses into the middle. Width will only be provided if your own team do not squeeze its own winger.

If the central defenders do not go wide to support the full back, the winger has more room to attack into the last third and from there, to manoeuvre a cross.

Wingers should vary their crosses. **Low, across the 6-yard box, produces most goals**.

As a winger, you are expected to chip in with your fair share of goals. A lot of these goals will come from attacking the far post late, making blindside runs as the team's other wide man puts it in the box.

You must **strive to get into the box with a late run to your nearest post every time** the ball is crossed in from the other side. Not to do so will deny you and the team many goal opportunities during a season and a fair few points.

You should occasionally consider shooting, rather than hitting a hopeful cross that is not aimed at anyone in particular. A left-footer playing on the right and vice versa provides opportunity to cut inside and let fly. **Play as a winger**, **think like a centre forward**.

Playing for Cambridge City in the early 80's, I had a manager called Bill Leivers, a former FA Cup winner with Manchester City. Bill advised me of what I might do *the first time* I get the ball around the attacking last third, facing the full back.

If I had nothing *definitely better* on, then I should smash the ball at the full back as hard as I could, aiming at his nether regions and disguising it as a speculative early cross. If I missed him, I should even try it again the next time.

The third time I received the ball, if I dummied to cross I was guaranteed a free run past the full back as he covered up, protecting himself from the cross. This time, I was to get my head up and make the next pass count.

I can't recall it resulting directly in a goal, but whenever I wanted a full back to back off a little and give me room to play, I knew what to do. Bill was a full back, he should know.

The winger's unit is his full back and a central midfielder. They are always there for him, offering support. When possession is lost, they squeeze together as the opposition attempt to play through their area.

11

Defensive Corners

Some managers prefer a defender on just one post. Some professional managers even have both posts vacant.

If I am the attacking team, I like to see that the defenders have an unguarded post. This fact convinces me that when defending, you should *have a defender on both posts*.

The amount of goals you see go in by a post where there is no defender should be evidence enough, and yet managers and teams of the highest level often opt for an unmarked post.

I cannot think of a better place for a zonal defender to stand.

The players chosen to guard the posts are normally not those you would choose to compete in the aerial battles of a corner, but **players** who would be **quick to react to any second ball** falling in their vicinity; full backs and wingers, for example.

Sometimes you see players resting on the post as if they don't believe that the ball will come anywhere near them, so they can therefore relax.

Everybody, whether attacking or defending a corner, **must believe that this corner kick or second ball is coming to him**, as only then will he be prepared to act if the chance arises.

Another key defensive position for me is the edge of the 6-yard box nearest to the corner taker. David Beckham would always take this position for his various teams. A tall, experienced player should play this role.

Tall because he needs to clear any ball low enough for him to reach, before it passes his position to be attacked by the opposing forwards.

He needs experience to be aware of any opposing players timing a run past him from his blindside, attempting to flick the shorter corner kick on.

If the ball is high and he cannot get a clean header directly away, he should attempt to get a really big-headed flick on it, to take it over everybody and away from the goal on the far side.

This is a key defensive position. If it is done right it means the attacking team must place the corner either high enough to clear this man, or wide enough of him to take it towards the penalty spot. More quality is demanded of the corner kick.

If it comes over higher, it is more difficult for the attackers to get a downward header on it. It is longer in the air and it is therefore easier for defenders to get underneath it, to clear.

It also becomes more available for the goalkeeper, who should have an advantage at corners hit high into the 6-yard box.

If it passes your 6-yard-box man on the penalty-spot side, it is at least in an area that puts more of the defending team between ball and goal and is a little far out for a successful first strike.

Claiming that near-post, first-contact position means that the opponents need to strike a decent delivery in. If you do not have a good man defending this position, even a poor low-struck corner can be a big problem.

The other defenders will have either a zonal or a man-for-man marking position.

Correct defence is always **a mixture of zonal marking and man marking**.

This is because you are ultimately protecting the goal which is a zone and playing bodyguard to the attackers is just one aspect of this.

Zonal is a starting point which puts you already in the vulnerable area we are trying to protect. From this prime position you are expected to react, which will mean **moving to challenge an opponent** who is moving onto the taken corner, within your zonal reach.

Known threats, such as big centre halves/forwards, should be taken man-for-man.

Make sure that the defender gets an equal, if not first, go at the corner, i.e. he remains goal-side and on the attacker's leading shoulder, and tries to read and stay a half pace ahead of the run.

The attacking runs should be *legally* impeded, basketball-fashion, by blocking runs, trying to remain goal-side and contesting any arriving ball.

The goal area is usually so congested and the runs so mazy that blocks are rarely, if ever, given as fouls, so long as the arms and hands are not too conspicuously used.

You cannot let yourself be out-muscled in your own box. If you are not paying attention, you will let the striker get the first *power move* on you and knock you out of your goal-side space.

Any pushing, pulling or general impeding should be done with the arms as low down as possible. Use your arm strength but keep arms low, aimed at the opponent's lower body. Most fouls given will involve arms and hands raised at least to chest height.

Competing with the forward and having some bodily contact with him as he prepares to head or strike the ball can affect the quality of his finish.

Moving a few paces to take some of the striker's space under the ball, even if you cannot jump and challenge for it yourself, is better than just watching the action unfold.

A free header or strike on goal is usually the more successful and what the defending team is hoping to avoid.

Zonally, there should be three defenders a few yards apart on the 6-yard-box line: one in the middle, and the others a yard inside the line of either post.

They should be in a position to read the taken corner and defend any ball that comes within their range. They change from zonal to touch-tight markers as soon as free attackers move into their zone. **The zone is just their starting point**. They are not rooted to the ground.

If another attacker blocks a defender who is marking one of the key opposition corner attackers and tracking his run towards the goal, it is the job of the nearest zonal, 6-yard-box defender to notice this and pick up this run instead. **You defend as a team**.

A defender should also defend the far-post six-yard box, making sure that they arrive at the far post goal-side of any attacker.

A defender on or around the penalty spot or 18-yard box is also useful, as a lot of dangerous second balls from poor clearances end up around here.

Once the corner comes over, it is important that the defenders continue to focus their attention on the player they were man-for-man marking or the zone they were covering, and continue to pick up any stray opposition players that may venture into it.

This is because **the second ball is often the move that ends up in the back of the net** rather than the first contact.

A defending team player can often switch-off as soon as he sees that the corner is not coming into his area, only to find it does so after a subsequent first-touch by either side.

The defenders should remain touch-tight to the attacker they are marking until the ball is cleared to a safe position; safe being in the defending team's possession or out of its last third.

As the ball leaves the 18-yard line, the defenders must quickly leave their goal area and push up, before the ball can be returned into the goal area by the attacking team.

They need to **win some territory back and clear some space for the goalkeeper**, whilst still keeping an eye on their opponents: leaving those opponents that remain in an offside position, but watching those that may still run through or turn from an onside position, as the ball is played back in.

Corner kicks matched with suitable attacking runs will always prove a problem and will always produce goals on a percentage of occasions.

Defending teams can improve their side of the percentage by setting themselves in positions which can react to most of the likely corner variations.

A belief in the importance of your role in the defensive set-up and the will to compete for the taken corner should make the defending team favourite the vast majority of times.

You cannot be stubbornly fixed to your position. These are all default starting positions, from which you *may need to react to the ball* and attack it.

Defending a corner can very easily lead to your own rewarding counter-attack, especially if the corner is claimed by the keeper, or a good clearance sets your edge-of-the-18-yard-box player away or finds the forward who remained up front.

In both cases, your attacking players must expand out of their own box *as quickly as possible to back-up your player on the ball*. **If they can attack quicker than the opposition can defend**, **you have a great chance to score**. See chapter 7, *Centre Midfielders*.

The key to defending corners is to stay alert, to react to and disrupt good movement; to attack the ball with intent, applying height and distance to any clearance.

12

Throw-Ins

Part of each foot can and must be either outside the touchline *or on the line*. The *point of release is not an issue* so long as the ball, held in both hands, is delivered from behind and over the head.

I hope that clears up two common misconceptions I hear and see regularly with throw-ins.

If you watch low-level local soccer, you will notice that a throw-in is usually an opportunity for the team defending it *to turn over* the ball.

It often results in the team taking it *losing possession*.

The main reason for this is that the team in possession squeezes the playing area into the man on the throw. The defending team then squeezes with them and you often get ten players in an 8-yard radius.

I have checked that fact out numerous times, at varying lower-league levels, as I always find it hard to believe in print until I see it again with my own eyes.

The ball is thrown into this compacted area and possession of it is equally contested by both sides. Either side has as much chance as the other to come away with the ball.

At top professional level, a throw-in, particularly in central areas of the pitch, is rarely contested by the opposition and the ball is just returned side-wards or backwards into play.

This is because the opposition *prefer to keep their shape*, getting their midfield behind the ball rather than risk being caught out of position; they don't want to risk too many midfielders on the wrong side of the pitch or the ball, in the event of a successful throw.

They are aware that in central positions, the possibility of successfully turning over a throw-in against the movement, touch and intelligence of top professionals is low.

A throw-in is only seriously contested in the last third of the pitch. Here, possession can lead quickly to a goal-scoring opportunity and marking in the last third is much closer, in all situations.

The reason the professionals, as opposed to local-level players, retain possession from their central area throw-ins is due more to **maintaining their shape, combined with good movement**, than to a good throw and first touch.

Players should not squeeze their own teammate taking the throw. They should stay around 10-20 paces away. One player should be down the line behind the thrower and one down the line in front of the thrower.

One or two players should be square of the thrower. One of these, presumably a central midfielder, could start 10-15 paces away, and the other 15-20 paces.

All **other players maintain their given positions, keeping the team shape**, ready to deal with the ball when it comes out of the throw-in situation.

A typical movement would be that a player down the line in front of the thrower makes a run towards one of the central-midfield player's positions. The central midfielder at the same time makes his run down the line.

Another movement is that the central midfielder further away suddenly offers himself towards the thrower, at the same time as the player closest makes a run away.

Essentially, making synchronised runs that swap positions may enable one of them to receive the throw, having got a couple of yards of space from his marker.

Go long and spin to receive short and **come short to spin and receive long** are good throw-in movements at lower level, where they definitely won't let you simply throw the ball back into play.

The thrower can also suddenly turn around and throw it to a player that is 10-20 paces behind him, as he is rarely well marked. If this player does receive the ball, he has **a great opportunity to switch the play with a long diagonal ball**.

At local level, this can often catch the opposition out, having placed a lot of their team too close to the throw in a vain attempt to turn-over possession.

A version of this in defensive areas is the **throw volley**. Here, the thrower throws the ball in to one of his players at a height that can be volleyed away, also providing a sudden switch of play into a less congested area or at least into the opposition's defensive line.

The thrower is also key to maintaining possession. Apart from delivering the throw that matches a run, he is also temporarily unmarked.

He must make himself available to receive a possible first-time return ball, whilst already having an idea in his mind of how to progress the move.

Third-man-running moves are also perfect for the throw-in. A player makes a run that is obviously not the object of the throw, only to be fed-in first time by the actual ball recipient.

When players **start their movement from distance**, **larger angles are created** in which to successfully throw the ball and it becomes almost impossible for the opposition to close down the space.

The rest of the team maintain position, providing width and space to play, so that if the throw is successful the team shape is ready to move the ball quickly through the structure and stage an attack; or at least continue possession.

If your team cannot do this then you should **work the line**. This means throwing the ball as far as you can, one yard inside and down the line, forcing the opposition to knock the ball out of play and moving your side further up the pitch.

Long throws have always been effective and have had a recent revival as an attacking tactic at the highest level of soccer; in particular, with Rory Delap of the Premier League.

I can remember Chelsea using the same tactic successfully with Ian Hutchinson in the early 70s.

Defending and attacking positions for long throws in the attacking last third are more or less the same as suggested in the chapters on corner kicks.

With a throw-in, defending teams are often slow to take up as defensive a position as they would were it a corner. Even around the halfway line, you sometimes see teams in defensive positions, as if it were possible to be offside from a throw-in.

In this case, they are open for the quick, long throw behind. **Your long-throw expert must also have a creative streak**, if you are really to profit from his talent.

A long throw, such as Rory Delap has perfected, is often *more successful than a corner*.

As opposed to the deadline corner kick, it comes from an angle that means it can be thrown into the goal, so that only slight contact is needed to keep it going goal-ward bound. Unlike a corner kick, a goal cannot be scored directly from a throw-in.

The trajectory of the long throw-in is often flatter than a corner kick and really removes the goalkeeper's advantage as favourite for the high ball.

It is usually more accurate and consistent than the normal corner kick would be. This means training-ground routines can be applied with more certainty that the delivery will match the movement.

If you are fortunate enough to have a long-throw specialist in your team, one tactic I recommend in local soccer is not using the long-throw option until it can be used to create a real goal-scoring opportunity.

The **first long throw has that added surprise value** that can catch the defending team out.

Another tactic is to hide exactly how long the throw may be. This entails throwing the first one or two short, looking for near-post runs and flick-ons. Then, with the third throw, have three or four attackers trying to drag the defenders as short as the nearside 6-yard box.

The thrower then delivers his biggest possible throw, which can sail over the near-post melee of players to be met by one of your best headers in a late run towards the middle of the goal.

If the opponents retreat, expecting a long throw, a teammate suddenly coming short can get the thrower back on the ball and a move started; or the cross can now be delivered by foot.

In all dead-ball situations, try to use the age-old elements of attack: **surprise**, **speed of movement and accurate delivery**.

Keeping possession from a throw-in is not difficult and in most cases should be a simple act of returning the ball into play; a simple restart.

The main thing is to get players to keep their distance, and to time and combine their runs, with the rest of the players maintaining the team shape.

Throw-ins are such a frequent occurrence that not using them to your advantage is a massive waste of good possession.

Make sure you have somebody taking throws on each sideline who can not only **throw the ball correctly and accurately**, but also has **a playmaker's eye for a quick or clever pass**.

A quick or disguised throw and a timed run, aided by the "no offside" rule, can create many a goal chance in local soccer.

There is such a thing as **a good throw-taker** and I don't just mean long throws. Get him on the ball, and relieve your bad throw-taker from this duty: you will be rewarded.

The key to good throw-ins is delivery, set up and movement.

13

Attacking Corners

Corners will always provide a good opportunity to score. The ball can be dropped into an area very close to the goal, thronged with moving players, and can be in the back of the net in an instant through any combination of luck, skill or incompetence.

The attacking team set-up is designed to overcome the strong defensive cover of the defending team, as detailed in chapter 11, *Defensive Corners*.

The manager should designate a main corner-taker for each side of the pitch. This should be **somebody who has a good**, **clean strike of a dead ball**. It may be a left footer from the right side and vice versa. Variation is to be recommended.

The point is to put a ball into the 18-yard box with pace and a little effect, resulting in the ball bending or dipping.

A ball pumped up into the air without pace or a dip or curl will make the keeper favourite to claim it at its highest point.

With a predictable flight path and landing zone, defenders are also likely to attack the ball in numbers, blocking any attempt by the attacking team to get underneath it.

If the attacker does arrive first, it is difficult for him to generate any pace with his attempt from this lifeless ball.

A fast-spinning corner kick gives defenders less time and information to get to its landing zone and nullify any attempts on goal.

Since the attackers are leading with their runs, they have a better chance of getting lucky and running on to such a ball before the defenders can react.

Setting your players out to attack a corner is really a matter of having your **attackers vary their runs**, so they cover as many of the possible landing zones for the corner as they can.

Most of the runs should come from deep. These three or four players should run in various directions and depths, starting between the 18-yard-box line and the penalty spot.

By depth, it is meant that these three or four players should not come in one wave, in one line; they should start their runs at different moments, and at different speeds and approach angles.

One may almost reach the goal line, one the 6-yard box, and a couple may only be 8 to 10 yards out.

This should ensure the average corner does not go behind or in front of all of your attacker's runs. A variety of flick-ons, flick-backs and second-ball incidences are catered for.

The variations of runs are innumerable. You can even have attackers that stand on the goal line and then make a run to the 6-yard-box line. **Movement creates**.

One attacker may run from a deeper position to a position in front of the defender guarding the near-post, 6-yard-box area. If he times this right, he can arrive blindside of the defender and just before the ball. He can then flick the ball on towards the goal or into the danger area for the **second wave of corner attackers**.

I always believe you should post a man in front of the goalkeeper. This usually attracts a defender and between the two, the space for a goalkeeper to come and claim a corner is greatly reduced.

It is not a pleasant spot to stand in, but the very fact that goalkeepers push and shove such a player shows that they are unsettled and fear a restriction in their view of, or path to, the ball.

In addition, many first contacts of the ball head straight for the centre of the goal. These often fall into the grateful arms of the goalkeeper.

If the striker taking up this position manages to stay alert and adjusts his position to remain between the keeper and this second ball, he may have an easy chance presented to him. He flicks the goal-bound first attempt into the net before the keeper can claim it.

Defenders are adept at impeding forwards by blocking runs and disrupting a clean jump or strike at the ball. Forwards can do likewise.

Attackers can employ this tactic to free another attacker from his marker.

An attacker may suddenly move between the defending centre half and the forward he is trying to mark, let us say your best header of a corner ball.

By timing this right, he can legally block the defender's run as he attempts to track the forward. **A corner is a team attack** and attackers should be up there to create a problem for the defence, *no matter whether the ball can come to them or not.*

All attackers, if they cannot get to the flight of a corner kick, should look at the possibility of blocking a defender's path to it.

This includes getting in the way of a keeper's path to the ball by quite legally reading the position to take up, and doing so before it becomes a deliberate obstruction.

As an attacker, you may need to create a bit of room around yourself. Use your arms (unseen, held low, strong and wide) and body strength to block a defender, holding him off to protect your space, from within which you can attack the ball.

I am not advocating foul play, but it is amazing what you can get away with in the 18-yard box, especially before the ball arrives.

By that I mean fair shoulders, backing and leaning in, taking a defender's desired space by easing him out of it with your arms (again held low) and your body strength, before claiming the ball for yourself.

Use both your upper-body and lower-body strength to muscle into a space. This is all generally tolerated, when there is no obvious barging or pushing with the arms.

A well-flighted corner or cross, combined with a good attacking run, will always prove a problem and will always produce goals on a percentage of occasions.

Attacking teams can improve their side of the percentage by setting themselves in **starting positions where they can react** to most of the likely corner variations.

A belief in your ability to make a run and jump that will compete for the taken corner is paramount. **Believe that this ball will come to your run** and that you will get a good contact on it and you will be surprised at how ready you are if the ball does arrive.

Heading the ball at attacking corners requires technical skill, belief in your movement and bravery. Defenders can head the ball more or less anywhere and can protect themselves better. The attacker seeks to get his forehead on the ball in a controlled fashion.

Good goal-attacking headers of the ball in local soccer are rare and it is a real plus if you have any. I do not know how you teach this skill at our level, but it is very impressive to see a player with good attacking-heading ability, leaping like a salmon, laying passes and making attempts at goal, as if they had a boot on their forehead.

I remember seeing a ball hanging from a beam in a gym by a string through its lace. The ball would be swinging and the player had to jump high and head the ball with his forehead at the lowest point of the pendulum motion.

Maybe heading ability left the local game a bit when they took the lace out of the balls. We can all only try our best and, with a positive attitude, we might just get lucky.

As in so many soccer situations, in attacking a corner, movement is the key. **Movement distracts and disrupts the defence**, and with belief and luck, you could just run onto the perfect cross. Expect to do so; don't be surprised to do so.

Quick, **short corners are an option** if the defenders are not paying attention or have switched off and are not reacting; as is the low pullback to outside the box for the first-time strike.

Here the shot-taker, presumably only outside the 18-yard box to cover the counter-attack, feigns disinterest so as not to attract a marker.

A short corner can also be to a player who pretends to stay back, covering the remaining attacker(s), but then makes a sudden run towards the taker and the corner edge of the 18-yard box.

If successful, it can result in a shot looking for the far corner of the goal; or the corner-taker back on the ball after a wall pass and running in to box; or at least a closer, more accurate and dangerous cross from a better angle.

Alertness, as at all dead-ball situations, is key.

The paid variety of soccer is streets ahead in attacking corners and this is certainly an aspect lower-level soccer can improve upon.

Time, personnel and training-facility restraints restrict the lower league's opportunity to practise corners. Pre-season work, if the team personnel remain virtually constant, can instil the attacking and defensive corner set-up for the whole season.

If needs must, it is also an approach that can be put into players' heads in a dressing room before kickoff. **If players can see it in their minds, they can do it on the pitch**.

A team must be aware that its own offensive corner can quickly turn into a counter-attack for the opposition. The attacking team now has many players out of position and needs to bear this in mind when setting up for the corner.

The defending team will normally defend in numbers as well, so a quick break sees them as short of attacking numbers as the corner-takers are now short of defenders.

At least one of your centre halves would normally go up for a corner, being usually strong headers of the ball. His place at the back should be taken by one of your quicker players, who are not needed for the corner itself.

The first line of defence against the counter-attack is the player hovering 10 to 15 yards outside the box, ready to pounce on a shorter clearance.

It is usually enough to leave just two covering defenders up by the halfway line.

The quick one marks the usual lone attacker *goal-side*, giving himself enough space to have a clear advantage in reaching any sudden, long, overhead clearance.

The other defender marks the *attacker's front*, also giving himself enough space to reach any shorter clearance first.

Their priority is, **firstly, to delay any counter-attack situation** that may arise, until their own players can get back behind the ball; **secondly, to stop it** if they can. **Safety first**.

Each player is given his role in attacking corners in the dressing room, if not earlier on the training ground. It is even better if he always has the same position, as practice should improve how he carries his role out.

The player needs to understand that it is a percentage thing, where results will show over time, not every time. He needs to stick to his allotted role and believe in it and positive things will happen.

The key to attacking corners is good delivery, positional set-up, sharp thinking, diverse team movement and real intent

14

Free Kicks

Free kicks lead to goals. In the attacking last third, they are a free chance to have a shot at goal or to put a dangerous cross into the goal area.

Elsewhere on the pitch, they can relieve pressure and turn defence into attack.

They are a good thing to be awarded and a bad thing to concede.

Defending free kicks

I remember playing in the 80s in Germany in a decent local league. I was playing up front and was new to the German ways.

At one point in the second half, the opposition sweeper dribbled the ball past me, around the halfway line. I was surprised to see the manager jumping up and down on the touchline, cursing me for letting him past.

At full time, he had calmed down a bit and explained to me that I should never let a sweeper run free into our half. I should have fouled him, obstruction being the preferred means.

He said that in Germany, you **foul early**. That means **high up the pitch**, before the move becomes established and where the referee will let you off.

You do not let the move develop to the point where you need to make a foul near to your goal or, even worse, you never get the chance again. You make a small push or obstruction, preferably before the move gets into your half, and disrupt it.

In this way, the opponents are not allowed to build up momentum, but keep having to start again with all your men repositioned.

With a good modern referee, this tactic should not go unpunished to the degree necessary to keep it effective, but I still see it at work, now and again, at all levels.

Since I am not a fan of cynical play, especially at unpaid level, I will state that conceding free kicks is a burden on a team and they should be, as much as possible, avoided.

I have no statistics to back this up, but I would believe that the top teams in any league receive more free kicks than they concede, and vice versa for the bottom clubs.

Most fouls are deliberate, or negligent to a degree that renders them so. I am not talking about the rare genuine challenges that are harshly punished, but about the standard obvious pushes, pulls, obstructions, kicks and trips.

It can be heartbreaking for a manager to see his wingers or forwards give away free kicks when they are well placed in the attacking last third.

The defenders are under pressure, worried about conceding possession near their goal and desperate to get a clearance on the ball.

Suddenly that pressure is lifted by your own player committing a usually careless, if not downright stupid and needless, foul. This is an indication that your player is not clear in his own head about what he should be trying to do.

Or worse, he believes that it is acceptable to blatantly commit egotistical acts to the detriment of his own team.

Attackers should be aware that defenders are going to take the first chance they get to highlight the slightest of foul play. They will shield the ball and shove or pull you, whilst responding to any shove or tug back by going over.

This is because referees find it easier to give fouls to defenders in the last third for obvious *human* reasons. **Keep your arms off them and the pressure on them**. The defence may be desperate, but the attack should be composed.

The attackers need to be clever and stay calm, hindering any easy clearances whilst not giving the defenders an excuse to cry *foul*.

The longer the ball stays in the attacking last third, through the defence not getting a decent clearance on it, the greater the opportunity for creating a goal chance.

Partial clearances, made under pressure from the attackers, while resisting the temptation to foul, can be quickly returned to the danger area whilst your men are still present.

Soccer consists of many small incidents that build up to give a favourable or unfavourable result. Giving free kicks away in your attacking last third may seem insignificant, but combined with other small mistakes it will lead to goals against, instead of goals for.

Avoidable free kicks are setbacks and are unnecessary incidents that you can fix.

Conceding free kicks around the middle of the pitch is the norm. They are by nature mostly cynical, because if you want to break up an opposition move and are willing to accept the punishment, this is where you would choose to do it.

The central third is where teams choose to do battle. It is where the ball is, most of the time. It is the chosen point, where a move is no longer tolerated and a stand is made.

You should attempt to win possession here, where the risks of a foul tackle are outweighed by the potential psychological and positional rewards of emerging with the ball.

In the central third, players may feel safer being a little more, let us say, ambitious in their tackling, aware that a goal-chance leading directly from a conceded free kick is remote.

Players are expected to make challenges in the middle third position and their technique is so often exposed as deficient. This results, very often, in a lazy and impatient tackle.

They challenge from the wrong angle and telegraph their intent.

They should **put in the running to get into a good position** before making their tackle attempt.

They often tackle sideways-on, but from slightly behind the player as they chase him. This gives the attacker a good chance of touching the ball away from the incoming tackle or to put his own body between the tackle and the ball, drawing the free kick.

If they cannot get slightly ahead of the player, or have more speed than him on execution of the challenge, then they would be better advised to resist the attempted tackle, get goal-side first and begin their defending again.

If too many fouls are given away, the momentum is with the other side and sooner or later that will pay off.

Fouls are more likely these days to attract cards. Finishing a game with less than eleven men and missing suspended players next match is an issue, particularly in the professional game.

In the local level game, fines for cards can eat up the scarce club cash and puts a monetary value on the indiscipline that destroys many a small team.

The manager's standard response in light of this is to attack the referees, protecting their own players and ultimately themselves from criticism. See chapter 16, *Referees*.

Conceding fee kicks in your own last third is a more serious matter.

It is strange how many silly challenges you see, even at the highest level: needless penalties and 20 to 25-yard free kicks.

The overriding objective should always be not to tackle the opponent (egoistic objective), but to prevent his team from scoring a goal (team objective).

This should usually involve staying on your feet and blocking the entrance to the danger areas, resorting to a tackle when the opportunity presents itself and definitely when it demands it.

That must mean when the probability of making that challenge without giving away a free kick or being beaten is unmistakeably in your favour. This, while factoring in your tackling ability.

Otherwise, the move is allowed to continue as a better, safer chance to stop it may appear, even if it is nearer the goal.

You surely cannot be serving the team objective by giving away a penalty or edge-of-the-box free kick. They may delay the goal-chance moment and yet make it more likely to occur.

In the heat of the moment, when the heart is pounding and the stakes are high, challenges are made, and later regretted, that lead to these situations.

This is not to ignore the cynical fouls, which seemed like a good idea at the time but can lead to a sending-off and eventual goal.

The conclusion has to be that conceding free kicks, wherever on the pitch, is not a worthwhile policy to pursue.

If it is not a policy but an individual failing, then it should be rooted out.

I am not sure that a "no foul" policy has ever been genuinely pursued by any decent manager, such is and always was the number of fouls in a typical match. So I may be mistaken in this conclusion, arising mainly as it does from my dislike of the disruption to the flow of the game that is caused by innumerable tolerated petty fouls. Some given, some not.

Against my distinct instructions, the foul has been conceded! Now what do we do?

After **a foul, conceded in the attacking last third**, it looks possible that you may be caught short defensively by the quick taking of the free kick. This must be *innocently hampered*.

This is usually done by backing slowly away 10 yards and blocking the desired pass, whilst buying time discussing the incident with the referee or the opponent.

Meanwhile, the rest of your team are streaming back into and around their halfway area, making sure that the runs of the opponent's expanding units of players, starting with those nearest your goal, are covered.

Successfully delayed and once back in position, the game continues, with the usual two defensive lines of four facing the play.

This is almost the same **in the central third area**, except this time you should be in a pretty good defensive set-up already. If not, quickly assume one, using the same free-kick-hampering style as before.

In the professional game, most free kicks for minor, disruptive-type fouls in central areas will be attempts to carry on that same move, as quickly as possible.

A short pass keeps the previously achieved momentum going. These, like centre-field throw-ins, are simple restarts and are not considered to be of any tactical advantage in themselves.

In the local game, this central-area free kick is often used to put a ball into the opponent's 18-yard box. This entails the defence taking up a provisional stand on the 18-yard-box line. The goalkeeper positions himself just inside his 6-yard box.

The defensive line will drop back only if necessary and as the ball is played. This way, they give the forwards a chance to run obviously offside; and they only retreat after confirming that the ball is over them and runs from onside require them to do so.

This disciplined holding of the line, dictated by the depth of the free kick and not by the premature runs of the attackers, also creates time and a clear space for the goalkeeper to decide whether he should come for the free kick or drop and let the defence cope with it.

Free kicks inside the defensive last third, where the goals are scored, require a wall. The wall is there to deny a direct shot or to hinder the trajectory of a cross from the wings.

One or two men are usually enough to obstruct the line of a cross, especially as most of the players will be required in the box to stop the attackers from getting on the end of it.

Here, most of the features of chapter 11, *Defensive Corners*, apply.

Defensive last-third free kicks in central areas require heightened and immediate vigilance.

You must have a man stand in front of the player with the ball *immediately* after the free kick is given. He should deflect attention from his "excessively delaying" the taking of the free kick by mildly disputing the decision, asking the ref for time to create a wall, pointing to the correct position for the free, and other nonsense.

However, he should back away quickly as soon as his purpose is achieved to avoid a card.

Meanwhile, the rest of the team must not switch off.

A successful, quick free kick, taking advantage of the "no whistle needed" rule, seeks to catch the defence with a relaxed guard, taking for granted a drawn-out, dead-ball situation.

If *the attackers demand* 10 yards, then the *whistle must be blown* and a wall can be constructed. A wall 30-18 yards out can include three to six players, depending on the proximity and angle of the free kick and the preference of the goalkeeper.

The goalkeeper and one player should, between them, line up the wall so it shields a large part of, and at least one side of, the goal from the direct shot.

Allow for and hopefully deter the application of bend by providing an extra man on the edge of the wall, covering even the outside of the wall's post.

The tallest players should be positioned in the wall, favouring the near side not covered by the keeper.

The goalkeeper protects the exposed target area, with one eye on the body language of the free-taker for clues as to which route he will take.

He should shift his weight from foot to foot so as not to be easily wrong-footed.

Those in the wall have different concerns.

They should protect their family jewels with one hand, their nose with the other, stand tall, broad and brave, and tense themselves ready to take one for the team.

The outside member of the wall needs to be ever-conscious that a direct shot may not be taken. Instead, a lay-off might be made in an attempt to open the angle and bypass the wall.

In such a case, they need to respond by helping to fill this new angle with their frames.

There should already be another player or two on the correct side of the wall expecting this eventuality, ready to charge the recipient of the laid-off pass.

This is also **the basic set-up for an indirect free kick**, as a direct free kick is always potentially a pass; the only difference being that the wall and goalkeeper know in advance it will not be a direct shot and may consider adjusting their positions to cover the most likely laid-off angle.

Adaptations, like getting the wall to jump at the same time to combat the known threat of a dipping-ball specialist, are definitely better left for the professionals. The risk here is that jumping produces more gaps than it fills.

I have often seen an experienced player, at the last moment, back away to the post covered by the wall, psychologically deterring the kicker from picking that post. Even if he subsequently moves, it may affect the free-kick execution.

He can also remain to head the ball over if necessary, but must not attract the opposition to take up similar positions, especially those that unsight your goalie.

A well-taken free kick in the last third will always create a problem.

If not directly unstoppable, these are decisive seconds when the defensive ability of your team, en masse, will be severely tested. Luck combined with intelligent, brave and athletic goal defence will be your saviour. The best defence is not to concede the free kick.

Attacking free kicks

A sudden turnover of the ball, through receiving a free-kick decision in your **defensive last third**, occasionally provides an opportunity to catch the opponents top-heavy and short at the back.

If you can take the kick quickly, you may be able to hit an open space where a quick forward who has not helped out in the defensive phase can pick up the ball.

Or, you may deliver a short free to set a player with penetration ability off into the central third, seeking to find his forward in space.

This speedy counter-attack puts the opposition defence on the run; they back away to their last third, where they have to draw a line and can defend easier with fewer numbers. As they hold you up here, they give their own players a chance to get back amongst you.

Your own team has expanded out quickly in support of the ball, and now is the time to calm down and **take advantage of the space you have so quickly won**.

Consolidation of good possession and a more measured probing of the attacking last third, through pass-and-move, can now ensue.

You will not often have the opportunity to take such rewarding quick free kicks, but you must always be on the lookout for them.

The difference in speed of thought and mental sharpness between higher- and lower-level sides is never as evident as in dead-ball situations.

Inattentive players take this as an excuse to switch off and relax for a few seconds. Good players recognise these seconds as their opportunity.

More frequently in the local-league game, a free kick won in your defensive last third will result in a chance to vacate this danger area and move into and around the opposition's half.

The goalie, to take advantage of the offside rule and if he has a decent kick, should deliver this ball. The full backs go high up the touchline and the two centre halves slowly follow the ball out as it goes deep into the opposition's half.

The team sets up just like for a goal kick. See chapter 1, *Team Shape*.

In the central third, professionals may take a succession of quick free kicks to keep up momentum and set the move rolling again. At local level, I believe we should take the opportunity, *almost always*, to put the ball in the box.

Such is the reality of the lower standard of possession maintenance that more chances will be created by putting the ball directly into the last third, than by seeking to create better possession in there by building up through pass-and-move.

You will get enough chances in normal play to pursue pass-and-move without using up free kicks to do so.

In open play, this book advocates maintaining possession and passing and moving in order to get your players, in good possession, into the attacking last third. This is pure theory.

When you get *a free chance* to place your players up into the attacking last third without having to play their way in, *you should take it.*

This is even more the policy when you have somebody who can deliver a good testing ball into the danger area; a delivery that finds your men or turns the defenders, setting them off moving towards their own goal.

The players who have been given a free ticket into the attacking last third should now try to win possession of the ball and create a chance.

Free kicks awarded to your side **within the attacking last third**, along with all of the other dead-ball situations, are potential goals.

It may be called a *free kick* but somebody is going to pay.

Every local team should have two players who are adept at getting a 20-yard-plus free kick, up and down and on target. These should be hard enough or well-placed enough to trouble the keeper. One player might be a left-footer and the other a right-footer.

I believe they should share the free-kick-taking. They should both set up for each kick, so that the keeper is not sure which one will take it.

To establish this doubt, one may make a dummy run, even up and over the ball, aiming at one side of the goal, quickly followed by the actual taker who kicks to the other side.

This strike on goal is about **technique and confidence: confidence to trust in your technique**.

David Beckham, Ronaldo et al have their technique so well-rehearsed and ingrained that it can stand up to the most intense pressure. A weak technique is more susceptible to a negative thought. **You must believe you will score** and commit to the strike.

Imagine the shot you are going to take, visualise it happening and then *just do it.*

Laid-off and indirect free kicks are usually simple, because they only need to be simple. Even professionals find it hard to repeat complex training-ground-choreographed dead balls.

If more things can go wrong, more things will go wrong. A simple lay-off pass, which nullifies the wall, and a well-timed strike are all that is required.

A free kick that hits the wall, or otherwise ends up in play with the opposition, leaves your team vulnerable. At least one player around the dead ball should be thinking of the counter-attack and of the players in this wall suddenly charging away with the ball.

There should always be two or three players left at the back ready for a sudden loss of possession and a counter attack. See chapter 13, *Attacking Corners*.

Some players are accomplished at winning free kicks. "Diving is all about honesty. If you can fake that, you've got it made."

Some go down at the slightest contact. Some have made an art of getting their body at the last second between a *genuine tackle* and the ball.

Some blatantly seek out this contact, hanging a leg or straying far off the ball. They seem to foul the defender and yet get the free kick. Some do not even need the contact to go down.

If he is your player, then he is clever; if he is opposition, then he is a cheat.

Soccer mirrors life and there is a lot of hypocrisy out there. We say one thing and do another.

15

Training

I take it for granted that all the players mentioned in the previous "position" chapters of the book have a certain standard of fitness. This is essential, if the pass-and-move theory is to work well in practice.

Unfit players cheat. They cheat in little areas of the game that they hope will go unnoticed.

A major reason why the professionals can provide the multiple movements necessary to set up the triangles of support, which sustain possession and enable penetration in numbers into the attacking last third, is their physical fitness.

Unfit local-league players will seek to save their energy. They will use it when they have to and not until they have to. They will use it after the chance to play good soccer is gone.

Since good movement is pre-emptive and speculative, and the running is in advance of any obvious need for it, good movement is the first thing they cut.

Good movement is the key to pass-and-move, and unfit players will not provide it to any decent standard — no matter how fit their soccer brains.

Therefore, physical fitness gives you a massive competitive edge over your opposition at the lower levels of soccer. If your team is fitter, it will provide more options, outlets and support for the man on the ball. Your ball possession and thus, chances to score, will increase.

In fact, get them in shape, on and off the pitch, and insist on a little pass-and-move, and you should have no problem winning regularly in your local-level league.

That is all most of the lower-level professional teams do. They take the youngest, more able players, get them fit and teach them the basics before they develop too many bad habits.

You can do the same to a less gifted but committed group of players.

In the professional game, all players should be fit. If they are full-time and injury-free, there is no excuse for them being otherwise.

It is taken as a given that fitness is the first thing you must bring with you on match day. Here, **the will to win is important, but the will to prepare is compulsory**.

The competitive edge gained by professionals by being fitter than the opposition is negligible. Their competitive edge is to be found elsewhere, in honing techniques, tactics, and teamwork.

In the lower-local leagues, fitness is a rarity.

If some players are gym instructors, sports teachers or have some kind of job or healthy lifestyle that keeps them fit, then maybe. They will have a massive personal advantage on local-league match day that they would not have in the paid game.

The average standard of fitness is not very high. Many players are overweight. This translates to a team's inability to play soccer to the level it and its manager would wish.

This means that no matter how well-intentioned players go out to play the pass-and-move game they may have in their head, I would be surprised if they managed to do it to any degree for even 20 minutes.

When a player is tired, his concentration and soccer brain are affected. These often shut down first, before the running and technical ability.

Being fit is the difference between getting into the right position or standing in the wrong position, because you are either saving your breath or recovering it.

It is sad but true that **the best thing you could do for your team's performance is improve its fitness**. A fit team against a generally unfit team should win every time.

Appropriately, the most difficult task and the biggest challenge you have is getting modern-day, local-level players fit. Fortunately, most local-level teams have the same problem.

Local-league training, going back at least 20 years, offered a very different style of match preparation than that practised today. The main emphasis then was on aerobic fitness, with running and circuit training taking up the bulk of coaching time.

This, combined with less available fast food, and less sedentary lifestyles and jobs produced a leaner, fitter, local-league soccer player. You can easily see this by comparing clubhouse photos of the same local teams, going back 30 years.

There were fewer distractions for young men in those days and joining a soccer team would be the focus of their social life. Now, it may be just one of a number of leisure activities they pursue.

On the up side, they get to watch more good soccer and receive more expert, detailed, soccer analysis than was ever previously possible. They hear, and have access to, a lot of soccer knowledge; unfortunately, you need to be fit to use most of it effectively.

Technique and tactical awareness that are not fitness-driven have certainly improved over the years.

Soccer is still a running game though, and you can't be a good player with a bad player's lungs and legs. **If you are fit and strong you get to use your ability, but not unless**.

Thirty years ago, technical soccer knowledge was less prevalent in local soccer. There was hardly any soccer on the TV. Information on training routines was scarce and any knowledge that was available was passed down via the often limited experience of older local-level players and managers.

Training drills, props, bibs and balls were not as readily or cheaply available.

Blend this with a game that was arguably more physical, and it is understandable that a large *emphasis was on physical training*.

The competitive edge you might strive for in those days was a quicker direct style, with a tougher battling spine to the team. Those attributes needed to be steely-fit.

The modern local soccer player has many more distractions and some of these are dietary. Self-discipline is difficult with today's lifestyles. I do not believe you can get lower-league-level youngsters to do the sort of training their predecessors would have done.

I have set many a youngster off on laps of the field to find that most cannot keep up a moderate pace — this would not have happened in the past.

Generalising here, young adults have a problem pushing themselves physically as much as the older lads would have done.

They do not seem to show any hesitation in dropping out or slowing right down when they consider it is too hard for them. The old macho peer pressure, along with the respect given to the trainer and the discipline meted out by the trainer in a training session, are no longer so evident.

Thus, the **training methods have evolved** to make use of the increased technical knowledge within the local game and the reduced willingness to work hard (run) in the sessions.

There are many great training drills available in books and on the Internet. Many local league-level clubs have trainers, with and without coaching badges, who have great knowledge of them and use them extensively in the sessions.

These drills are a product of modern sport pedagogy and aim to **isolate a necessary skill or action and repeat it**, until it hopefully becomes part of the instinct of the player.

These drills can combine two or three skills with a certain amount of running sneaked in between them. At best, they practice a move relevant to the weekend game.

I particularly like the speed dribbling between cones over a reasonable distance, using both feet. I like the pass-and-move drills at speed between cones over a reasonable distance.

I like the heading ones and the trap-and-pass ones at speed between cones. I like the ones that flex and stretch parts of the player's physique, thereby promoting the necessary physical agility needed in the game.

In short, I like the simple training drills that target a routine match skill or movement and include a sprint or two with limited recovery time.

I don't like involved drills that take ages to explain or have players standing around for long periods waiting their turn. I don't like slow-paced drills or wasted minutes of confusion as players do them wrong, due to their complexity.

Such drills are a godsend to those lazy, unfit players who would hang around *stretching* all evening if they were let. They are not enough for the player that wants to work hard.

Many of these complicated drills come from the professional game or children's soccer camps, where the drills must be mentally stimulating, constantly changing and fun.

Professionals spend a lot of time on a training field. Sometimes they need to be entertained and mentally stimulated, just like the children.

New drills of various complexity and seriousness are always welcome to break up the tedium of the standard, physical, humdrum session that can be a professional's working day.

They are already fit. These drills can easily keep their fitness levels topped-up.

Many of these drills are frills, time-fillers and conducted for bonding purposes.

I do not believe they can serve the same useful purpose at local-league level, no matter how professional they might make the trainer and players feel.

Good for bonding they still might be, but the fact is the local league-level player's biggest problem is that he is not fit. Like any unfit person, the remedy he least wants to hear is that the cure is exercise. He would rather invest in a new lighter pair of boots to help him run faster than do extra sprint training.

If players do not want to run, then we must include a good portion of running within drills. They are here to work. **Try to keep them moving**. They should do press-ups, star jumps, slow running on the spot, or at least stretch and shake the body out when between drills.

A local-level club does well if it can hold two midweek evening training sessions of one and a half hours each week. This time is precious. It should not be squandered standing about or leisurely doing half-paced drills that flatter to deceive.

Hard work pays off in the future. Laziness pays off now, that is true, but the more valuable weekend pay-off is what we are attempting to earn on training nights.

I know players who never miss a training session and yet are so unfit at weekends you would despair. It is very hard nowadays to push people to put in enough effort so that they might see some reward.

It may be hard to get people fit in two one-and-a-half-hour sessions, but if they are not willing to push themselves, and if they stop at the first sign of their heart beating quickly and their lungs breathing heavily, you have no chance.

How do they expect to run the 8 kilometres-plus necessary in a match? The answer is, they don't. If they can't do it in training, they will only *pretend* to do it on match day.

If they are tired during a normal match, it is not because of what they have done during the game, it is because of what they have not done in training beforehand.

The beep test, at any time in the season, will assess a player's fitness and show you and him clearly any fitness deficit he may have. Make sure players don't cheat.

Running ability and recovery time will expose the unfit, not the weighing scales. Muscle weighs more than fat. The heart is a muscle and it needs to be exercised to grow strong.

You need players with a strong heart.

The players will have different levels of fitness, but they will all need to work to the peak of their *own physical ability*. Some need to be pushed. "As little as possible" will be the default position of the lazy individual unless nagged at by his mother or partner — or in this case, you.

In a perfect world, players would arrive at training already fit. Fitness is a way of life. Good health is a lifestyle. You will still need to keep yourself fit long after you give up playing soccer.

Sometimes I hear unfit players moaning that training can't be hard enough because they are still not fit. They forget about how they spend the other days and evenings of the week that are not training nights.

As if three hours of light exercise and a weekend match played at their own comfortable pace could ever compensate for the overeating and other sedentary indulgences they allow themselves. They say they want to get fit. What are they on, a 5-year plan?

Why don't they go for a run, a warm-up and sprints on the occasional non-training day or go to the gym for a session or two? Go for a bike ride or press-ups and stationary exercises at home.

Their body is theirs; it does not belong to the soccer club. Why do they expect the club to get it fit for them?

The soccer player's body should be a temple, not a rundown community centre. If they really want to improve at soccer, the message is simple: get fitter.

Training, if players came to sessions fit, would be about sharpening their overall soccer fitness, honing skills, bonding with teammates, forging team ideals and experimenting with playing styles.

Training for local-level clubs should serve a variety of purposes.

It can maintain fitness. It cannot provide fitness.

It can sharpen to the required match pace. But a certain level of fitness is a prerequisite.

It bonds players. They get a chance to mix and communicate, away from the stresses and time constraints of match day.

The coach and managers can introduce, emphasise and explain the desired playing philosophy to the players. They can do this through drills and through conversations with the squad as a whole, to a unit of players and to individuals.

Individuals can be assessed. Your fittest, quickest and most technically gifted players are adjudged, as are the most unfit, slowest and least ball-friendly.

You should not wait for match day to find these things out.

You can also assess character.

Some players are great in training and not on match day. This is usually to do with inordinate confidence when amongst their club mates dipping to zero confidence with strangers.

They are prone, if this is their character trait, to treat the strangers/ opposition with undue respect, as if they were technically better or physically stronger than their team. They display a fear of the unknown.

Some players are average at training and regular stars on match day. These people respond to a challenge and need to be motivated to be effective. They can only look good when giving 100% and that is not often advisable in training.

Whatever a person's character, it is revealed on the soccer pitch — see chapter 18, *The Manager*; and the combination of training and match day will tease it out.

Soccer does not build character, it exposes it, and over a season you should eliminate the weak ones from your team.

You can adapt your training and talks to help individuals that have a deficit and seek to improve them. Look for a player's strengths in training and consider how best to use them on match day. Work on an individual or team weakness in the drills.

A technical player who can make the ball sing in training may not know when to use his skills in a competitive match. He has to learn when and where to use them. You can work to improve his understanding of his position and his knowledge of the game.

A fast player may not know when is the best time to use his speed or how to receive the ball more often or stay onside. You have time in training to get inside an individual's soccer head.

Give confidence to some, stir up a few, calm down others.

You can save time on match day by going through parts of what might be your team talk in advance. Sometimes, it is good that players have a strategy in their heads a couple of days before they are supposed to implement it.

A typical, valuable, training session for me would consist of simple and continuous exercises designed to **hammer home the never-changing basic principles of soccer**.

It is a game of sharp thought and movement, requiring a deft technique, suitable character and running performance; a game that demands instant and informed decisions.

Include a warm-up of maybe 20 minutes to get the heart pumping, lungs blowing and to dissipate any stiffness of joint and muscle. Backward running, side to side and knees-up etc can all be part of this period. Shake all muscle fibres loose, rotate all joints; let gravity do its work from neck through to shoulders and arms, hips to legs, knees and ankles.

Get warm and sweating before any stops and stretches. Everything in your body is connected. You cannot isolate one part of your body and stretch it. You need to warm up and loosen the lot. Slow stretches held in position over time aid flexibility.

You can have some of your chats at this stage. Team bonding is facilitated during the stretches and slow jogging, as the weekend's stories are told.

Then switch to a succession of running drills, through the paces up to full sprint. The limited recovery here is vital. **Get the heartbeat up**, **down and back up again**.

Sprint, recovery and repetition are the ways you will discover and enhance the running capability of your squad and individuals.

The team's state of fitness will determine how long this period can last, but 30 intense minutes should provide a good session. Make sure the tempo is kept up, and the required sprint speed and recovery times are enforced.

Place equally paced individuals or rivals beside each other to add a competitive edge, if possible.

Idle and unfit players will try to hide in the numbers here. They cannot hide at the weekend.

That is why it is better to have a trainer putting them through the hoops and a manager observing. The trainer is too involved in the action and can be cheated. The manager can observe individuals and the players never know when he is watching.

The levels will waiver from player to player and session to session, but you will get to know the acceptable level. This is where discipline in a club is paramount. Without discipline in a club, you are literally wasting your breath.

Have a period of drills, including press-ups and sit-ups, in the downtime.

Having two trainers is great for keeping up the tempo as one can be setting up a drill whilst the other conducts one. These drills will involve all ball-related techniques demanded in the game, performed at near-game pace.

Training must relate to the competitive game to be of value. Running certainly relates. The emphasis must be on quality of training rather than quantity. It is amazing what a disciplined squad can achieve in an hour.

To finish the session, games should be set up to practice pass-and-move and keep ball.

Constant nagging by the manager and coach to keep standards up and do the right thing, the percentage thing, is a necessary stick to wield if the players are going to learn from these training games.

If they are unguided, the game can sink into an undisciplined kick-around that will have no relevance to match day. These kick-arounds cultivate bad habits instead of good ones.

Split the team up, with experience against youth, and you will usually see the old lads triumph. Mix the teams and you will get the best quality matches. The experienced lads should be doing your coaching in these games for you.

Three-touch is a realistic game scenario to play. Players should preferably use one or two touches *if the moment allows*. There should already be many one-touch drills in the session, but a three-touch maximum allows practice of the bread-and-butter game technique.

One touch controls the ball. A second touch, if required, moves the ball into your own safer possession, to shield it, to lose or beat a marker, to get your head up and/or to open an angle. The third touch passes the ball from this new improved position.

Three touches should always be enough to move the ball on if the movement is adequate, and this scenario is more relevant to match day than enforcing a one-touch or two-touch maximum rule.

In fact, it would be the second touch as described above that I would be looking to improve for local league-level match day.

You will find on match day at this level that the ball can be a hot potato and the norm is moving the ball on as quickly as possible, as if the game was a race.

Players kick it forward, as soon as or before they have trapped it, without the second touch that is often necessary to buy yourself time, to get your head up, to pick a proper pass.

The opposite is also common: taking too many touches, just because you can, before deciding what you want to do — the dreaded *bad fourth touch*.

This may involve running with the ball, until stopped by the opposition, instead of choosing your own moment to stop when you could still take advantage of any ground gained.

A keep-ball game, where there are no goals and the object is ball possession, is good practice for keeping shape, i.e. spreading out over the pitch and pass-and-move.

It is good for contracting on to the ball to squeeze possession out of an opposition that have not expanded quickly enough, and then to expand your own shape to fill the area once the ball is won.

Having no direction, i.e. no goal to play towards, teaches players to stop, turn around, and keep possession by going in a different and unexpected direction.

They can practice the skills of turning around whilst on the ball and exploiting the space behind and square of them; the skill of protecting and shielding the ball, putting the body at a side-on angle between the ball and the opponent.

These are skills not commonly enough seen at local-league matches.

When watching and commentating on these games, always concentrate on the movement more than the passing. Encourage cleverness, feints and hard work to lose a marker and make an angle for the man on the ball. The man on the ball is King.

You must insist at the end of a good ball session that **this standard be achieved at the weekend and not left on the training field**. Not to reproduce training form on match day is often a cowardly act, showing a lack of belief.

The team has to be brave and confident to perform the same way against the opposition as it would against its own on training nights.

It is amazing what physical fitness does for your bravery and self-belief.

A warm-down of a few minutes at the end of a session helps shake the muscle fibres loose and free up joints. It enables last managerial checks on fitness and availability; a chance for last advice to the players in preparation for the weekend's game.

If you are lucky enough to have lights and use of a full-size, all-weather training pitch, you will be able to practice dead balls and game situations throughout the season.

You will also be able to target your goalkeepers for specialised training sessions and focus on any weaknesses they, and indeed the team individually and as a whole, may have.

There are many good free soccer drills available online, all designed to teach some fundamental technique, playing style, move or strategy.

I wanted this book to exercise the soccer brain by thinking about what it is we are *actually* trying to do. This involves visualising a moment in the game and breaking it down into its component parts, then putting it together again on the pitch in our minds.

If you can see it in your mind, you begin to believe you can do it on the pitch.

Training drills can subliminally impart this knowledge and since this is a chapter on training, I will suggest one. This drill encourages the two fundamental concepts: number one, shape, and number two, pass-and-move. It is particularly suitable for a pre-season session.

On a full-size pitch, you set out your 4-4-2 formation, in the *correct shape for your goal kick*, and you start play from your goal kick. See **goal kick** in the *Team Shape* chapter.

The opponents are only six in number.

Two of them can only harass your defence and must stay between your midfield line of four and your goalkeeper.

Three of them can harass the midfield, but not the forwards or the defence.

One of them can challenge your two forwards, and stays between them and your midfield.

You take your goal kick and the object is to play the ball quickly through all positions, whilst maintaining possession away from your six opponents, so that you *eventually* end up in good possession in the attacking last third.

Short passing is preferred. Execute long forward passes, long switch balls or a dribble only when necessary. The players must understand the point of the drill if they are to *keep it realistic.* Keep the tempo up.

The team should try to pass the ball from left back through the defensive structure (round the houses), up the right wing to the forwards and back. The team should try to involve all players whilst keeping its shape.

The shape only contorts as it manipulates the ball through its area.

The team can move up until your central defenders are on the halfway line, and at least four of your players are on the ball in good possession in the attacking last third.

They have mimicked the shape of a good team in possession of the ball.

Job done, start again.

If the opponents turn the ball over, they have won, and you must start at the goal kick again.

This should help teach players to maintain the correct shape in possession and:

To maintain their width and open angles.

Not to get too close to each other on the ball.

To pass and move. To communicate and combine their movements.

To support your unit of players as the ball passes through your area.

That the strikers should make themselves available and help the midfield play themselves into the attacking last third.

To take their time, not on the ball, but in attacking into the last third. It is more productive to do so when you have sufficient numbers up and ready to dart into that area.

That **the game is not a race**. To be patient. It is the quality of the attacking move we are seeking to improve, not the quantity. That security in possession leads to more numbers in the attacking last third and better chance creation.

To move up in a controlled fashion as a team with its shape intact.

To understand why we need the correct shape and how we maintain it through the provision of angles and distance, so that pass-and-move can spring from it. How this shape and pass-and-move can get you far up the pitch without losing control of the play.

That the team is now ready to switch from risk-averse possession maintenance to speculation and individual creation, as you control the ball into the attacking last third.

Ready to implement one of the three ways to score in open play. Which is another practice session.

16

Referees

"Careless" (free kick), "reckless" (yellow card), "using excessive force" (red card), and "unsporting behaviour" (yellow card) are all FIFA terms used to measure the gravity of offences, listed in their "Laws of the game".

With the massive expansion of television coverage of matches and the slow-motion analysis of controversial decisions, the position of referee has become a hot topic in the professional game, where vast amounts of money can hang on the blow of a whistle.

Media soccer pundits are particularly critical of the man in the middle.

You rarely hear a supportive voice for a referee who has made a judgement contrary to the view of the match analyst.

The television companies would love to use their technology and experts to referee parts of the game. That would make their influence on the professional game even greater than it already is.

In the professional game, goal-line technology is a possibility, as whether or not the ball has crossed the line is a technical, objective fact. If the referee could be made quickly aware of this fact, it would be one polemic decision less for him to make.

FIFA are looking at goal-line technology but to date, still have to come up with a satisfactory, seamless and cost-effective solution. When they find one, it will no doubt, be introduced.

Offside is often a technical fact, and would presumably require a fifth official viewing a screen with a playback and freeze-frame facility.

FIFA is wary of delaying the game's decision-making process as, in practice, the game must continue until a decision is made to stop it.

The length of time the referee would have to wait to be told the decision for each offside or goal-line incident could affect the free-flowing nature of the game.

Another major incident could take place between the pending decision and the offside or goal-line incident that provoked it. You could have two incidents awaiting video evidence.

There are complications involved that will only come to light in practice and before that happens; the effect on the game can only be imagined.

Technology for fouls, handballs and other false-refereeing decisions is, I believe, a non-runner as there are so many of these, all over the pitch, that to deliberate on each one would detract from the free-flowing, spontaneous game of sudden change that is the game we love.

Many **such incidents are subjective** rather than technical in nature, so that the person viewing the screen has a decision to make that may cause as much controversy as the original refereeing decision.

Even technical fouls and refereeing mistakes, that there can be no argument about, can prove a dilemma.

If, for example, a handball penalty is awarded by TV evidence to one team, then the opponents might justifiably point to an earlier penalty incident they could have had in their favour.

There are always incidents in the 18-yard area, just as much foul play as a handball, which are not dealt with by the officials but are caught on camera.

Sometimes in the penalty area at corners, there are various fouls going on for and against both teams. What should video evidence or, indeed, the referee without video evidence decide here? Deciding which foul takes precedence is subjective.

The rules seem to pass the buck or accept defeat, as they dictate drop ball if both teams are simultaneously committing equally ranked fouls.

In reality, the referee ignores them all equally or picks the foul most serious or the one nearest to the ball.

A goal is disallowed by video evidence because an attacking player handballed it, before the goal was scored. The attacking team may claim that previous video evidence, minutes before, proves an unpunished foul, in open play, before one of the opposition's goals.

If that foul had been given then, that exact goal could not have arisen.

The choice for video evidence would seem to be either for a completely level playing field, you **correct all missed fouls and false decisions equally**; or select only major penalty area, "game-changing" bad decisions and amend on a subjective basis.

If the game were allowed to proceed, as the infringement or mistake is at the time considered not *game changing*, that decision by the fifth official not to fix the mistake could itself become a major mistake if a short time later, it leads to a *game-changing* moment, to the advantage of the team that got away with the decision.

In effect, all of a referee's decisions are potentially *game changing*. For example, a player unaccountably avoids a second yellow card for a clearly "reckless" foul and later in the game scores the winner. A throw-in mistakenly given the wrong way at one end could lead to a goal at the other.

How do you fix these *game-changing* refereeing errors?

Are they errors or just *alternative subjective decisions*?

Ultimately, the video committee or fifth official's decision could be as subjective and divisive as that of the original referee, which was given without the aid of video replay technology.

Slow motion can make a foul look like an inconsequential contact, when in real life a slight touch on an opponent at full-pelt is enough to send him tumbling.

"I think the action replay showed it to be worse than it actually was."

In real life, I have never seen anything happen in slow motion. Why pretend that it does?

The possible, practical, difficult scenarios with video adjudication of the game seem endless. If it were to be brought in without those scenarios being properly explored and thought through, it could damage the game severely as a live spectator and participative sport.

The football authorities are wary of giving television companies, who control the necessary camera technology, the power to control games — and not just for cost reasons.

They already use it for pursuing players for actions that were off the ball or missed by the officials. For grave offences, this is to be recommended and may be a portent of things to come. Again, **consistency will be the stumbling block**.

If video technology (goal-line incidents excepted) were to be consulted for *normal*, open-play refereeing decisions, it would be another degree of separation between the local game and the televised edition.

If the trend for this continues, the armchair spectator and the local active soccer player will become as remote from each other as to be fans of two different sports.

This could lead to young children giving up the game in disappointment, after discovering it is not the same as on the television. No slow-motion replays and perfect hindsight decisions, just subjective and opinionated real time.

In my opinion, the television pundits pushing video evidence (again goal-line incidents excepted) have missed the fundamental significance of the referee and assistants in the game...at all levels.

The trouble with referees is that they do not seem to care who wins.

The referee is not infallible. He is not meant to be infallible. He is meant to be impartial.

One of the fascinations of the game is the element of luck involved in it. Without this, it would be a lot less watchable and a less-exciting game. It would lose some of its magic unpredictability.

You might always get a dodgy penalty in the last minute. Great!

You might give one away. Bad luck!

A video committee, stop-starting the game with a lot of boring reversals of petty decisions or the subjective selection of what constitutes a "major" bad decision to overrule, would take from the spontaneity and unpredictability of this great game.

It may just result in controversial decisions by the video committee and not now by the referee.

One of the most important phrases in the rules of the game is, "**if in the opinion of the referee**..." This phrase for me is crucial and should be inserted more often than it actually is in the rulebook. It sometimes says, "**if the referee considers**..." and I do believe it is implicit in all of the written laws of the game.

It's not about what you think you saw, it's about what the referee thinks he saw.

Having played in, managed or closely watched more than one thousand live local games of soccer at varying standard levels, I appreciate the reality of this proviso.

At the basement level of local soccer and *at its worst*, you may get an ageing, unfit male referee who has never played competitively and is in it either for the tax-free petty cash and/or to vent his frustrations on players and managers alike.

They try to ref the game from the centre circle and make vindictive decisions arising from their burnout, as a result of years of abuse suffered at the hands of players, managers and supporters.

You may get their younger counterparts, who although genuinely and enthusiastically trying their best, have no real grasp of what they are seeing. These are the younger referees en route to stage two and burnout.

However, they are "the ref" and it is **their considered opinion that counts**.

If you accept this, you can move on from confronting the ref to attempting to influence the ref, which, depending on his character type, are two separate things.

Refereeing is by its nature difficult. You cannot see everything. Some things are a matter of interpretation or line of sight, and players will con you if they can.

I remember playing golf for the first time with a bunch of footballers, recent converts to the game. I noticed players reporting a wrong score, improving their lies and replacing their ball nearer the hole once marked.

The principle I took from this was that footballers are used to having a referee to enforce the laws of the game. In their eyes, it is okay to bend the rules when nobody is looking and they can get away with it. That is the referee's job to sort out.

Bending and breaking the rules, conning or let's call it cheating, appear to be an accepted part of the game of football. The person who has to limit its *rewarding effect* for its perpetrators and on the result of a game is the referee.

There are many borderline decisions made during a game. Most are subjective.

Is it a foul or a fair challenge? Handball or accidental? Backing in or a push? Actively offside or not interfering or gaining an advantage? A fair shoulder or tackle or "careless", "reckless" or "using excessive force"?

The referee's decision depends on his line of sight, his experience of the game, the relative importance of the match, his mindset on the individual involved or on the team/management in general, the state of play, state of the pitch and state of his private life.

The referee for me is not separate to the game. He is part of the game. Just like the wind and the rain, the surface of the pitch and the vagaries of chance, he will influence the game.

The proof he is part of the game is that **if the ball strikes him, we must play on**.

Not only that, he has a licence within the rules to influence the game, because of the "if in the opinion of the referee..." or "if the referee considers..." clauses.

Managers never complain when they have been wrongly awarded a throw-in, corner, free kick, penalty or the benefit of an offside decision. Or if one of their opponents is harshly sent off.

They fail always to see the hypocrisy of their behaviour.

For me, the referee and his assistants are stars of the game, as much as your centre forward or goalkeeper. They can certainly influence the game as much.

If we could just get it collectively into our heads that it doesn't matter what we saw or think we saw, it only matters what the refereeing team thinks, we could move on from one blow of the whistle to the next, cursing or praising *our luck*.

Luck is an important feature in the game of football. The best team may eventually win a league, but over 90 minutes a favourable or unfavourable (not right or wrong) decision can change a game and dictate a result.

You will always have players, fans and management appealing for decisions in their favour, though they know it should go against them.

When a disputed decision goes in their favour, they readily accept it as an evening-up of previous decisions that have gone against them.

They never do the reverse calculation.

They should, for the sake of the game, cut out the hypocrisy and accept the fact that both sides want the ref to see it their way. The referee *will* hopefully see it his way, and not be unduly influenced by one side or the other. *If I agreed with you, we'd both be wrong.*

What infuriates players and managers is inconsistency.

Some refs might be frequent whistle blowers who stop play at every sign of infringement. Others may let more "rough" play go.

Some you can talk to and voice your disagreement with, and others will book you if you so much as look at them funny.

Players and managers can deal with these different refereeing styles if they are consistently applied throughout the match.

A lot of referee abuse derives from the partisan view that one side is being unfairly dealt with, if similar incidents are being handled in conflicting ways by the same referee, in the same game.

Decision-making can be improved and made more consistent by constantly improving the quality of the referees, especially in the professional game.

Incompetence and worse still, deliberate cheating or influencing of the game beyond the necessary and the normal, should be rooted out for the sake of fair play and the ordinary decent referee.

I must say, I have seldom seen deliberate cheating or malevolent influencing by a referee in my thousand-plus games. I have seen incompetence. I have seen considerably more incompetence in the playing standard affecting the result, than incompetent refereeing.

I have seen massive bust-ups over which side's throw-in it is on the halfway line, or over an offside whistle when the forward involved would never have caught the through-ball on a motorbike. I have seen a lot of deliberate cheating and malevolent influencing of the referee by players and management.

We, in the local game, have to accept a large part of the problem as regards respect for the referee. If all your players played as well as the ref refereed the game, you would more often than not be a happy manager.

The leadership in this regard must come from the management, who are often the worst offenders in referee abuse. I wonder sometimes when I see these managers shouting out their biased views of incidents in the game, exactly how they would referee it...

Not a pleasant thought for the opposition.

I have known local referees who, if you cultivate a friendly relationship with them, will often give your team the benefit in borderline decisions. Others seem to blow against you more, the nicer you get.

When managers and players moan and whinge at a ref throughout a game, you will see three types of result.

1. The ref will positively discriminate against them.

2. The ref will officiate neutrally and oblivious.

3. The ref will succumb to the pressure and gift them a decision.

When I see a player moaning excessively at a ref or about decisions, I see **a player looking for an excuse to lose**. The same goes for management. They are abdicating any responsibility they have to influence the result of the game and giving it to the referee.

So they can lose, but in their minds come out blameless.

The point is that refs are human. They have different personalities and their refereeing of a match will vary according to a myriad of factors relating to the human condition.

We should all just let them get on with it and accept the odd unfavourable decision as bad luck; no more deliberate than the unlucky deflection, or the blatant miss by your centre forward, or an opposition goal virtually thrown in by your own keeper. **Give me the strength to accept the things I cannot change**.

In professional refereeing, there is huge scope for improvement. They have the money and the time available to make sure they are at their best. They should have an eagle eye and be fit enough to put in sprints in a nonstop 90 minutes.

At best, they should have played at some respectable level, so that they get the playing view of things. They should have a flawless grasp of the laws. They should have man management skills and a cool, confident and strong persona.

They should feel supported in carrying out their task by all concerned. This should prevent the feelings of intimidation at crucial points in a game.

In the lower leagues, with a shortage of referees (pre-recession), we have to accept nearly all that offer their services. We, as managers, players and supporters should respect the right of referees to be in charge of decision-making, leaving management and players to be responsible for the quality of the football.

This would remove the most popular excuse for losing and make us take responsibility for the game's result. It might even, therefore, help improve the football.

In the professional game, ex-pros could be fast-tracked into professional refereeing, so long as they meet all current criteria as to ability and come through a short but rigorous testing and apprenticeship scheme.

They may bring that sometimes-missing quality of football common sense, through their knowledge and experience of the game, to typical match incidents.

It would also help referee-minded, lower-level pros who cannot afford to retire to continue to earn a living in the game they know so well.

I do not want to denigrate the many capable referees who have no credible, competitive, adult soccer-playing experience. Some people have good football knowledge with a limited exposure to the playing side of the game; and playing at a good level doesn't always translate into a good understanding of what you are seeing.

I am just pointing out that there must be plenty of ex-professionals out there who would be perfectly suited to a fast-track policy, if their refereeing ability was confirmed.

I only know of one Premier League referee who was a footballer at a respectable standard. Mark Halsey was a teammate and Cambridge City goalie in 1982. I believe he continued for a good while as a non-league player before starting to referee.

Mark is now fifty-plus and I am sure the experience gained playing a decent standard of local soccer helps him immensely with his refereeing, as much as does his maturity.

The age of referees in the pro game should be irrelevant, in the same way a player's age is irrelevant. The referee must regularly pass all fitness and performance quality tests. This would allow older people who have played until late in their careers to become referees.

The current model of the referee's career, beginning at school age and eventually becoming a professional referee after 10 to 20 years of coming up through the ranks, is, I believe, flawed.

Give me a referee who played 10 years as an adult before starting to referee any time. I know there are exceptions, and past players can also make bad referees, but a career referee from 16 years old? He may know the rules, but does he know the game?

Analysing refereeing decisions and vilifying them, to the point where they become vastly more important than all the bad misses and bad play during a game, is the TV presenter's and the losing manager's speciality.

That the referee is, week-in, week-out, likely to be the main reason given for losing is now a part of our football culture. It is endemic in football at all levels.

In other team contact sports, the degree and amount of referee criticism is less. Rugby, for example, does not have a culture of constantly seeking fault in the referee.

We should change that culture within our sport. This change should be led by FIFA and UEFA.

They can do this, firstly, with a conscious effort to raise the profile of, and respect for, referees; then, with directives to punish excessive dispute and non-acceptance of a referee's decision.

Yellow cards and red cards should be more common for such offences. The message has to be that the referee and his team is in charge of the decision-making during a game.

They are part of the game. They are there to mediate between two opposing forces. They are there to give their "considered and binding opinion" on incidents. **They are not there to provide scientifically proven facts, just definitive decisions**.

More importantly, the message is that it is not the players' or management's task to make decisions on possible rule breaches or game incidents.

Their duty is to deal with the decisions they receive by getting on with the game, regardless.

Just like they do if a *wrong* decision is given to their advantage.

The onus should be on improving refereeing standards and helping them in their decision-making where possible. For example, like the two extra 18-yard-box assistants at UEFA league games, or *instant goal-line* technology.

If there were enough yellow and red cards administered to combat excessive dispute, players and managers might learn that it is not in their interests to heatedly question decisions once made, but to get on with the game without receiving a card or losing a player.

In cases of abusive, excessively demonstrative or prolonged dispute, apart from the card, a free kick should be given, 10 yards nearer the goal than where the disputed incident occurred. If it was a disputed throw, an indirect free kick should be given instead of the throw-in.

Yellow cards and reds should be more prominent in the game for *deliberate* foul play. Fouling the opposition as a tactic to stop the move progressing is a frequently used ploy; and minor yet blatantly deliberate — and thus in my mind *unsporting behaviour* — fouls often go unpunished by a card.

They are considered by referees to be just "careless" (no card), even though they are cynically designed to stop that particular attacking move whilst allowing the defending team to regroup behind the ball. It doesn't matter that the move was in its infancy.

If you give a free kick away, that is a known threat and can be managed. If you let play run, you are into the unknown and chance. Cynical players and managers do not like the unknown or trusting to luck. They like the dice loaded in their favour.

They get time to reorganise and mark up tight, the right side of the ball. The attacking side loses whatever momentum they may have had and no card is shown. Why should a foul be systematically allowed to benefit the team that committed it?

The fact is that **the vast majority of fouls in a game are deliberate**. All the pushing, pulling and obstructions are mostly avoidable. The players commit them because they work. They hinder if not stop the opponent and are insignificantly punished, if at all.

The player that commits these fouls will often dispute them to the ref as part of the psychological battle, sowing doubt in the referee's mind, subtly implying favouritism and avoiding a card.

Some fouls are reckless examples of bad attitude. These fouls intimidate the opponent by presenting them with a chance to go for the ball and risk getting hurt, or leaving it for the "excessive force" tackle.

The overly aggressive tackler will always appeal to the ref that he was going for the ball; failing to see that if you go for a ball without due care and attention to the well-being of others in the game, then it is "reckless" (yellow card) or "using excessive force" (red card).

The defence for most foul play is, "I got the ball". As if you cannot commit a foul and get the ball at the same time. If they do get the ball, it is often only because they have intimidated the standing player from properly competing for it.

Every *cynical, blatant and deliberate foul*, no matter how non-dangerous it might be, warrants a card. These fouls are against the spirit of the game and deliberately flaunt the rules to gain advantage.

Non-dangerous and *non-advantageous fouls*, where an "accident" or "going for the ball" is at least a possibility and does not serve to reward the perpetrator's team, can be considered "careless" and punished enough with a free kick.

A card must follow for cumulative "careless" fouls.

A good tackle is a genuine attempt at the ball, not the man, and very few fouls are accidental.

Accidental, in that the tackler goes cleanly for the ball, not through or into the attacker, but is simply beaten to it, after underestimating the speed of his opponent or his own slowness.

Accidental coming together during or after a tackle, or in a 50/50, are rarely problems when both players go into the incident with genuine good faith and intentions.

One may be deemed to have fouled the other "carelessly", but with no deliberate intent. This is just a free kick.

Flailing and negligently trailing legs, kicks and heavy impacts into the opponent, despite having first touched the ball, are all "reckless" actions and a foul. Yellow card.

You are not allowed to get the ball and then the man. **If you cannot get the ball without getting the man, then you cannot get the ball**. You have to get into a position where you can go for the ball correctly. This is **the art of tackling**.

This does not mean that you cannot cause the opponent to fall over your challenge. It just means that your challenge gets the ball and does not continue into the opponent. **It is the opponent that continues into your successful challenge**.

I see nothing brave in flying in from distance against somebody running with a ball at speed. Who is braver, the player running upright and unprotected or the player that launches himself into him, with his boots leading first as his protection?

The aggrieved manager often says that if a man is sent off, it harms the game as a spectacle. I do not believe this. Indeed, 11 against 10, 9 or 8 can be quite a spectacle.

If it is helping to change attitudes and a fouling hypocritical culture into a fairer, more sporting one, then it is a welcome spectacle.

I have often seen a game suddenly clean up, after a couple of yellow cards and a red have been brandished. How can the bad tackles and excessive disputes wane in fear of another card, if they were not deliberate activities in the first place?

Pundits who hark back to the good old days when you could tackle from behind, cards hadn't been invented, and "when men were men" are definitely living in the past.

Good strong tackling always was, and still is, an art. Kicking people was always a foul. It was just tolerated more if the ball was involved.

The trouble is, now that a certain protection is being given to skilful players, *the art of tackling*, as opposed to recklessly challenging, is being exposed.

Not enough players have this *art*.

We must **encourage the fair charge**, *shoulder to shoulder* when both players are on the ball, seeking control using body strength, with firm arms held low to win and protect it.

We must **encourage the good**, **strong**, **brave**, **clean tackle** and the talent and timing it requires.

We should **target the reckless**, **negligent challenge** and the cynical, thuggish, bullying attitude it masks.

Soccer should be a contact sport, not a collision sport.

Deliberate or accidental handball is an unnecessarily subjective call for a referee. The guidelines for this decision could be cleared up. In field hockey, if the ball hits the foot it is a technical foul, regardless of whether it is deliberate or not.

Deliberate handball, in all instances, should remain a direct free kick.

If the ball hits an arm that is not tucked into the body, then it should *always* be deemed deliberate.

This would put the onus on the players to ensure their arms are not in a position where they could be struck *accidently* by a ball that would have gone past them.

Their arms now, when blocking a cross or shot, would need to be tucked close into their bodies. By into their bodies, I would guide the referee that "tucked in" means no gap between torso and arms whatsoever, i.e. the body and arm are touching, the whole length of the arm.

If the ball strikes the arm that is tucked into the side of the body or protecting the manhood or face, and there is *no movement to repel the ball from the body or control it with the arm or hand*, then this and this only should be judged "accidental".

The arm and hand in this case can be considered part of *the body* since they are not positioned away or separate from it.

You can now only block the ball with your legs, *the body* and your head, no longer "accidentally" with your arms — which, the advocators of accidental handball claim, you only have out for *balance* purposes.

If you don't want to risk handball, you have to risk being *unbalanced* as you challenge.

The result would be that incidences of arms and hands blocking crosses, through-balls and shots would decrease. The decision for the referee would be greatly simplified.

Handball would become a technical foul in all instances when the arms are away from the body. You would have to consciously prepare your body stance to avoid the ball with your arms and hands, or bear the consequences. Some players already do so.

The referee no longer has to ponder a player's intent. He only has to decide if the part of the arm struck was away from the body. If so, it is handball. If hands, elbows and arms are touching the body, then play on.

Sometimes a player attempts to trap the ball and makes such a mess of it that the ball strikes his own arm, accidently bringing it under control, and then he clears the ball as if nothing has happened. I am always amazed that this bad play can result in accidental handball and play goes on.

This rewarding of bad or careless play is ridiculous and removing most of the subjectivity from handball would solve the problem.

Now, of course, genuine accidents will be punished; but so what? The game is called football, not handball.

I always believed that if the laws were applied strictly, there would be many more penalties in a game and if this leads to more, well and good. We all love goals, just not against us.

Deliberate "accidental" handballs would become another negative and cynical action no longer rewarded. It would close down one more avenue of "accidental" cheating that contributes to the current hypocritical culture.

You cannot leave the advocacy of fair play and cultural change to the professional players and managers. They have a vested interest in immediate results and are under pressure to live selfishly, in the moment.

As one manager said: "Show me a good sport and I will show you a player I'm looking to sell."

If the professional game, through results, rewards managers and players for bending and abusing rules and referees, then many will. This is why you need a FIFA and a UEFA and national bodies, separate to the professionals within the game.

They should keep each other in order, but not be trusted to keep themselves in order.

The solution is to strengthen and clarify the rules and to politically support a referee's right to, occasionally, make bad assessments of an incident when enforcing those rules.

Negative aspects of the culture of the professional game seep down into the grassroots of local football. Some players and managers could not take their local weekend game more seriously if they were playing in a Champion's League final.

Foul play and cynical behaviour can go undetected in local matches where, unlike the pro game, there are no cameras, media or even spectators to adjudge and restrain it.

The overtaxed referee can struggle to contain a game when the attitudes are cynical and unsporting; where the locals mimic the professionals.

Local football needs help from the top down in changing this culture. The pro game needs to lead in making the game more attractive, physically safer and more skilful. Rewarding quality and honest play, and persecuting the cynical acts that seek to smother them.

Time-wasting by the corner flag is, for me, a negative part of the game that could be eliminated under existing laws (the "unsporting behaviour" rule).

Teams can quite properly waste time when the ball is in play. Keeping the ball and running the clock down is a skill that teams should acquire to see out narrow wins or hard-fought draws. If they want to waste time fairly, then they should do it in genuine open play.

Picking the ball up from pass-backs and excessive holding of the ball by the goalkeeper, before a kick out from his hands, were once valid ways of wasting time.

Rules were eventually introduced to deny this form of time-wasting because, not only was it boring and frustrating to watch, it was considered unfair to the result-chasing team. Although it was, in theory, open play, the opposition had no real, fair chance to get the ball.

When a player, or often two, **take a ball into the corner-flag area**, they are using a technical aspect of the pitch's shape and limitation to deny the opposition a fair chance of taking the ball from them, without committing a foul.

The opposition are not allowed to leave the pitch to tackle them from off it and there is no doubt that **the intention is to deliberately waste time**.

By using the corner triangle of the pitch, the time waster(s) is **unfairly wasting time**, using the technical restrictions of the field of play. That, in my opinion, is "unsporting behaviour".

As soon as the player deliberately seeks to waste time in *the immediate vicinity of the corner flag* (let's decree 2 yards), the whistle should blow and an indirect free kick awarded.

We have too many small unpunished fouls because they are *unpunished*. Pulls and pushes are especially tolerated. The rules need to be implemented.

Changing this would mean at least a season of lots of disruptive whistle blows and cards. Eventually, people would deem it not worthwhile to go for a ball they cannot fairly get, or to push or pull an opponent because they either believe it is worth the punishment or will go unpunished.

This cultural change, from tolerating certain types of intentional foul play to punishing it sufficiently enough to stop it, will not come easy. It will be resisted. It will cause upset. The change in attitude will only be gradual. *It is not likely to be attempted.*

We may need three yellows to make a red. We may need another colour card. If you are going to inflate the punishments, you will need new coinage.

Sin bins *might* be the move that deters the constant petty but effective fouling: sin bins as some version of an "orange" card, or for cumulative fouls by an individual or team.

The other face of the dirty coin of deliberate and reckless fouling is the diving and feigning injury to win fouls or get opponents carded.

It would have to be zero tolerance for these offences as well, offences that are notoriously hard to assess in real time.

Simulation offences provide scope for video-evidence punishment *after the match*. This type of video evidence should be encouraged because if simulation ever finds its way down to our level, *it is time to despair*.

There are many faults in the game concerning the abuse of the rules, time wasting and cheating. They are prevalent because they work in the favour of those committing them.

Changing the rules to prevent these faults and tinkering with the laws of the game is a path not to be pursued lightly. What we can do is enforce respect for those rules we have already.

First, it would be necessary to strengthen the hand of the referees. This would require a change in our attitude to football referees.

They need to be able to make genuine mistakes, because stamping down on these rule abuses would require frequent and subjective judgements being made in real time.

Referees will get it wrong sometimes.

We all need to **treat a referee's decision as a part of the game**, like the bounce of the ball or a deflection; it could go with you or against you.

Referees are the twenty-third player on the pitch and they do influence the ball.

Good luck, bad luck and human failings are fascinating elements of the game; and without them, football would not be the incredible worldwide phenomenon that it is.

Referees' faulty decisions fall into this category.

In football, good luck and bad luck do not always equal themselves out. Just like in life.

17

The Club

The management team at a local lower-level club consists of a team manager, trainer, physio, kit man, grounds man, secretary, fundraiser, treasurer, the committee and the tea maker. Depending on the club, this could be one and the same person.

At higher local-level standard, there will be more people available to the manager, and the local-level game owes a huge debt to all those volunteers who come together to provide a weekend's sport for the young adults involved.

As far as team affairs go, a management partnership consisting of a manager and an assistant manager, sharing the task, is very common.

Most technical aspects of this book, as regards the playing of the game, have relevance from the lower local leagues up to the higher local standard of *expenses-paid* soccer.

This chapter is more relevant to the grassroots of lower-league club and team management.

Teams, or better said, clubs, that have existed for some time, like any institution, will have a culture. This culture has evolved over the seasons.

It is a complex combination of past and present player, manager and committee-member attitudes, and values formed through past results, attainments and disappointments.

Their expectations of a manager's performance will be based on this culture: a culture formed within the limitation of the club's resources and location.

It is hard to change the culture of a club and any manager who tries to do so, rightly or wrongly, will meet stiff resistance.

The club culture, whether it involves playing style, discipline, training attitudes or administration, evolved for a reason and changing the culture to improve results is a long-term process.

Change will mean a walk through a minefield of small and occasionally big decisions.

In soccer, you cannot quickly change culture without changing the personnel. This is not always possible and it is very difficult to change an individual's attitude if it is ingrained in a fundamentally different culture.

Sometimes, you have to get on with what you have got. You have to insist on the parts of your philosophy or soccer theory that are not negotiable and drop the other stuff.

There are different ways of running a club and playing the game, and at times you will inherit administrative staff and players who are not amenable to your desired style.

One thing that will never change is that **you will always be judged on your results**.

You must focus on results from day one; because without them you will not be given the time to fully implement your own soccer vision. There will be no long-term cultural advance for the good of the club if you neglect the short term.

The short term demands tactical awareness, match strategy and man-management skills. Radical philosophical changes to playing styles are for the long term.

So, a local-level manager faces the problems or blessings of an existing culture at a local club. Let's assume he has a committee who believe in him and do not undermine his authority, a club secretary that supports him in his league and player dealings, and a management team in place to help him with his tasks.

Ideally, the manager would have an assistant manager. Also, a trainer, i.e. somebody (or two) who can put the team through their paces at least twice a week; a physio or sponge man; and a kit man or team help.

I have left the manager's sorry task to the last chapter in the book.

Kit man

You are doing well if you have one of these. Better-resourced clubs may have a washing machine and drying facilities in the clubhouse, but very often in the lowest leagues it is the manager's responsibility to wash the kit (or find someone else to do it).

The kit man often doubles up as the sponge man; he is sometimes, sadly, also the manager's assistant or, worse still, manager.

Some laundries do a good deal on washing kits. The money can come from the players' subs and you just need someone to bring the kit to the laundry and back to the changing room on match days.

It is not a good idea to have players alternately doing this, as they have a tendency not to turn up the week they are doing the kit — or just as likely, to turn up without the kit.

If you are a particularly hard-up team or understaffed, you should consider selling home-strip shorts and socks to regular team members at close to cost price.

They are then responsible for bringing these to each match and washing them afterwards. Fines for dirty kits may be necessary.

You can then bring fewer socks and shorts to match day, just enough to allow for those who have forgotten theirs (another fine or another pair sold) and for those new players yet to have purchased kit.

Result: less washing, more funds.

You need match balls and training balls; bibs and cones and raingear for the subs and management. Warm-up tops and bottoms, depending on your finances, can also be made the responsibility of the players, along the same lines as the socks and shorts.

As kit man, you are part of the team and in and out of the dressing room. You are part of the atmosphere and a cheery positive comment is always welcome. A few words of confidence to the younger players or even your own favourites never go amiss.

Bring a bin liner to place the dirty kit into, so you don't mess up the clean strip or kit bag. Bring other bin liners for any sideline equipment or baggage that should not get wet. Lay the shirt numbers out on the pegs, ready for the team.

The manager should consistently give the same squad numbers to the same players, saving time in getting the shirts and warm-up tops on and filling out the match card.

Physio or Sponge man

If the club has a volunteer qualified physio, it can be very beneficial. The players will be getting good advice on their injuries, and the club or players may save money on after-care.

Normally, however, an ex-player or somebody with physical team-sport experience will suffice. A caring demeanour would be nice as well, but if you are lucky enough to have a sponge man, be happy with what you have. Local-level volunteers are scarce.

They should make sure they have a decent medical bag, enough to administer antiseptic first-aid and protection to cuts and other superficial collision injuries.

It should contain chemical ice packs and bandages to treat sprains and swellings, and paracetamol and ibuprofen for minor pain symptoms.

Sundry other sprays, rubs, straps and tapes, tailored to the specific hypochondriacal needs of the players, complete this bag.

Thankfully, the overwhelming pre-match smell of deep heat, tiger balm, massage oils and liniments seems to have left the dressing room, along with the jock straps, no longer worn.

The bucket of cold water and the magic sponge may also be no more. The physio/sponge man is in charge of the water bottles and energy drinks and snacks.

Tricks of the trade might include taking energy drinks for players, and management information, onto the pitch during injuries; time wasting; and delivering subtle Machiavellian comments to the referee.

They should have a plan B ready for incidences that might involve serious first aid, ambulances and hospitals. A health insurance policy is a wise move for the active player.

RICE or rest, ice, compression and elevation are the best advice for the standard, frequently occurring, soccer injuries: strains, sprains and bruising. Players should buy two reusable warm/cold packs and some bandage from the chemist for self-treatment at home.

A lot of money can be spent on receiving this simple advice or service from professionals, who may relieve the swelling in your wallet at the same time.

Time is the best and most economic healer. Injuries should be given enough time to heal so they don't become chronic. If you play while carrying a knock or a strain, you run the risk of a compensatory injury. Training should be resumed before you play competitive matches.

Trainers – See Chapter 15, *Training*.

Assistant Manager

In the professional game, the famed management partnership of Brian Clough and Peter Taylor epitomised the success to be found in combining two very different managerial talents and coming up with a much more effective team governance.

Other examples of manager and assistant might be Kevin Keegan and Terry McDermott or Alex Ferguson and a succession of assistants.

In fact, in the professional game there is probably an assistant manager at all clubs, whatever his official title might be.

Nowhere is a manager's assistant more needed than in the lower-local leagues and not only to help carry the kit.

The assistant and manager must trust each other's personal integrity (as concerns their relationship), trust each other's soccer knowledge and awareness (as far as their allotted tasks go), and be totally at ease with one another.

The partnership will soon fail if hidden agendas are separately pursued or if one's position is being undermined by the other.

This is a hierarchical relationship and the manager's decisions must be final and acted upon, even if the assistant has misgivings about player choice, team tactics or other issues.

The assistant manager must be allowed to have his private say, but **a united front on the manager's decisions is to be presented to the team**.

The assistant can always blame the manager if decisions go wrong. The buck does not stop with him. The manager does not have that luxury.

The assistant not only brings another set of eyes and ears to management; he also hopefully brings with him managerial strengths that the manager may lack.

For example, the assistant may have a difference in character or outlook that stimulates and sharpens the thought processes in the manager's soccer brain.

The assistant may have an empathetic way with the players, whilst the manager may be, by nature, more direct and abrupt. This may manifest itself as a variation on the good cop/bad cop routine.

The assistant may be more defensive, whilst the manager has more of an attacking mindset.

He may be more tactically aware, whilst the manager might have a more philosophical approach in setting out and making game changes to his team.

He may favour, or be a better judge of, technically and more individually gifted players, whilst the manager judges character as a priority and lets discipline, team spirit and selflessness hold sway in his team selection.

He may be more prudent and the manager a risk taker.

He may relate to a distinct set of players, such as the attackers and the youngsters, whilst the manager is more on the wavelength of the experienced defence-minded players.

Whatever the qualities of each, it is the successful combining or the perfect dovetailing of both sets of abilities that makes **two better than one**.

Team talks can be shared before the game and at half-time. One can present the tactical coaching address, whilst the other covers the motivational mindset necessary for the impending game.

One can go around individually talking to each player and letting him know what is required of him. The other can address the back four or the separate team units, bonding them in their common and interchangeable tasks.

The assistant and the manager can bounce ideas off each other, sounding them out for feasibility before implementation. Manager is a lonely enough job without having a wingman to pitch ideas to and demand ideas from, when the going gets tough.

Being two shares the load in many ways. Not least for the benefit of your personal life, you can share training nights and have the odd weekend off.

In soccer, you really can use two pairs of eyes whilst watching a game. The assistant can concentrate on one individual for a while to see if he is performing satisfactorily, whilst the manager continues to watch the big picture.

The assistant might notice one of your team getting tired or a failing in another player's position. He might keep his eye on one of the opposition for a while, one of the opposition who is causing problems.

By watching him closely, the assistant might come up with a solution.

When he relays this to the manager, the manager can then have a quick look at it, whilst the assistant keeps his eye on the big picture. In this way, **they can see the whole game and small detailed parts of that game**, which may have a big influence as the match progresses.

Substitutions and tactical changes are all made easier for the manager by having a knowledgeable assistant beside him, and the management pair is to be recommended at all levels of the game.

Indeed, at the top level it is the only game in town.

18

The Manager

Much of this chapter describes a theory of management. As in all chapters of this book, the theory is what we might strive to achieve, the practice is what we end up with.

The closer the two converge, the better for the quality of the team and the fulfilment of those in and around it.

Theory is positive thinking; practice is what happens in the meantime.

Positive thinking is the key to success in everything.

Players at the lower levels need to be advised constantly on the theory of soccer.

They particularly need to be aware of the theory relevant to frequently occurring aspects of the game, such as goalkeeper kicks, corners, throw-ins and free kicks.

You might think that better opponents are much better than you in open play. They may well be; but they are certainly much better in the 100-plus dead-ball/restart situations from which they begin to impose their open play game upon you.

Knowing what to do or being told what to do, even repeatedly, does not mean your players will try to do it. That is where good man management comes in.

You can be spouting perfect soccer theory, selecting the correct tactics and team, but if you do not know how to present it or win people over to it, you will not be able to implement it.

Man management, the ability to capture hearts and minds, to convince people, to bring them with you, **is worth so much more than all the strategies and systems**. I don't think you can get that knowledge from a soccer book, certainly not from this one.

There are three reasons why our players might let us down: **ignorance, apathy and inability. Don't know, don't care and can't**. We can show them the way. We can motivate them and we can work on their fitness, technique and tactical awareness.

First, you need to get them on your side. You need to create the pictures in their heads, so that they also believe in the value of employing the theory. You need to use the theory to eliminate failures and the mistakes before they get you eliminated.

The trouble with soccer is that it can be difficult to score a goal and you cannot win on points.

If there were lots of points or goals up for grabs in a game, then surely the best team wins.

In soccer you can play the beautiful game, employing large parts of the theory, dominating possession and creating many chances. Yet the opposition can keep it tight and long ball, and win one-nil, scoring their only chance against the run of play.

Like a stylish boxer against a one-trick puncher, you may look the most likely winner but end up losing the match.

In every game there are "if" moments. If the referee had given us that decision or if that chance would have gone in or gone wide. **Luck means a lot in soccer**. Not having a good centre forward or goalkeeper is bad luck. Not using the theory isn't.

Players will always make a wrong decision, mishit a pass, fall over or lose concentration to such an extent that the theory appears redundant in the heat of the game. It can certainly appear abandoned when a match deteriorates into individual battles.

Nevertheless, soccer theory is a good guide to start with. The cold sterile theory will never change, but will always prove elusive.

There is an opponent involved amongst many other factors, which means **pragmatism is the managerial trait that trumps the theory** every time.

It is how you and your players apply elements of soccer theory, whilst facing up to the realities of the local game and all its restraints, that will determine the results gained from it.

If you are lucky enough to have better individual players than your opponents, then you already have a great chance, even with minimum use of the theory. It is already by nature hard to score, so set your team up as hard to score against and away you go.

That is one reason why the theory is ignored or not enforced at the lower levels. Until you play a team at a significantly higher level, you never need too much of it to compete quite happily.

The theory takes time, **patience and hard work to instil**. Many choose not to bother, concentrating instead on just a few basics.

Let's get back to being positive and imagine a manager who is new to a club and fully motivated.

The manager should have an overall soccer philosophy or distinct way of seeing the game.

This can be simplified as **predominantly attack** or **defence-minded**; risk-oriented or cautious.

Naturally, the state of play dictates. All managers are, at times, both of these things, but the starting tendency leans one way or the other.

His ideology binds the team components into a functioning unit, striving to implement his chosen method of achieving the favourable match result.

He should pick his team to match that philosophy and instruct them consistently in what he expects them to do, in the key and frequently occurring aspects of the game.

He should make personnel and tactical changes necessary to ensure that his personal philosophy is progressed. This is within and outside of the match scenario.

There will always be crucial moments that will test his self-belief and game vision.

If the manager does not **fully believe in his own soccer philosophy**, then just as a compass goes wild at the magnetic pole, when subjected to extreme tensions his commitment to his ideals will waiver and he will be on the road to personal failure.

Your ideas are either good or they are not. **Everything else is man management**, including managing yourself.

Fail here, but not by failing to trust your ideas, ideals, philosophy or whatever you call your soccer knowledge that put you in this position in the first place.

If the manager is not picking his own team or directing his own style of play, how can he fully enjoy any fruits of success or feel any responsibility for failures?

Surely only a well-paid manager could endure being just a figurehead, having no positive match-affecting input into the team or playing someone else's game plan.

Soccer-team management, at the lower level, is largely an unappreciated, frustrating, time-consuming, and volunteering-type hobby.

It can have rewards in terms of recognition in the club hierarchy, results and performances.

The joys of being outside in the fresh air, being part of a team and giving something back to your sport are not insignificant.

To really enjoy it, though, you have to be true to yourself, pick your best team and tactics as *you* see them. If you fail, then you fail *on your terms*.

You can move on then, confident in the knowledge that you gave it your best shot and that you have learnt from many of the positive and negative experiences you have encountered.

Of course, you would have done some aspects of it differently, had you known then what you know now. That is **learning from experience**.

This is why a good manager is usually somebody with wide past experience in the game and/or in a management position.

Success is getting up one more time than you are knocked down.

You actually learn more from losing than you do from winning. Put simplistically, when you lose you analyse; when you win you celebrate.

If the team is losing regularly and you have just come in, you will need to batten down the hatches and battle. The players will not be up to learning anything too intricate, as their motivation and confidence will be low. A good recap of the basics may be required.

A manager should ideally look for **a captain who can be his manager on the pitch**. It is hard for a manager to make his instructions understood from the touchline.

The constant, instructive, orchestral-type conducting of the team's moves and responses are better coming from the centre of the pitch. Leading, as the manager cannot, by example.

The captain must be a good player, for he is the first name on the team sheet. He should not be injury-prone or inconsistent in performance level. If he cannot perform adequately and lead by example, it will diminish the effect he can have for you.

Choose him carefully and encourage his development. A good captain with leadership skills is a rare find in a squad and can be an invaluable aid to the implementation and enforcement of your chosen playing style or tactical set-up at any given time.

It can pay a manager to have his captain in one of the central positions. The captain should be the foundation that a team can be built upon. Central defence or the defensive midfield is the natural foundation for a team.

The central-defensive partnership, including the defending midfielder, determines a team's defensive success; and in a pass-and-move game plays a massive part in ball maintenance and dictating direction of play.

Therefore, both in directing early attack and late defence, a centre-half or defensive-midfield captain is perfect.

The manager should spend time with his captain, ensuring that the captain buys into his philosophy of the game and is willing to force implementation on the rest of the players.

Discipline matters here. Players, like children, need boundaries to feel secure and from within this security, to develop.

Sadly, if discipline is not part of the club culture, it is very difficult for a new manager to exercise it and it will prove a major challenge for him to introduce.

Without discipline, theory and practice too easily diverge. Self-discipline can make up for a lack in talent, but a lack of discipline will lay talent waste.

A local league-level manager will always be restricted by the players he has available and how much notice they are prepared to take of what he says. He cannot use money to replace players or motivate them to do things as he requests.

He has to cajole them, to bring them round to his way of thinking. He has to convince the spine of his team of the worth of his philosophy.

If he can control the captain and the dominant players, and has the full backing of his management staff, he has a chance.

As a manager, you will be fortunate if you have finished product or good raw material to work with. You may need to sign them or find the uncut diamond in your midst.

You need a solid, assured and dependable goalkeeper.

An experienced and resilient captain and central defender.

Keen, fit, talented players willing to look, listen and learn.

Pace and running ability on the wings, strength and consistency through the middle.

Each unit with the desired mix of pace and experience, creation and resistance.

Professionals are generally quicker, fitter and more technically gifted than local-level soccer players. The athletic gap seems to get bigger every season.

However, over the years I have seen many local soccer players who could easily match them if speed, fitness and technical ability were the only requirements.

The fact is the *mental side of the professional game* is leaps and bounds ahead of that of the local leagues. **This is what turns a technique into a game skill**. This is why a good ball juggler and athlete is not necessarily a good soccer player.

Patience, communication, concentration, anticipation, soccer wit and ultimately decision-making. All of a much higher calibre.

If those qualities came easy, we would all be playing good soccer.

Easy is what we at lower-league levels do. We want to turn up and play, without having to think too much about it or work too hard in preparation for it.

We don't want to tax our minds over what is just a game.

My contention, and a reason why there are no technical diagrams in this book, is: **if players can see it in their minds, they can do it on the pitch**.

This thought process is a little harder to achieve when players are not being paid or are not fully committed, playing purely as a temporary pastime.

They will not focus sufficient thought on the game to achieve a state of mind where the sense and purpose of a game's otherwise random events become clear.

Playing the game first in your head and then down on the ground requires concentration and thought processes akin to playing a massive outdoor game of chess against the clock.

They don't want to play chess. They want to run around unrestrained and let the ball do the thinking for them.

They basically have other things on their minds. Soccer should provide a physical challenge, not a mental one. They have been thinking all week, a game is time to relax.

They play soccer to socialise with their friends, compete with their peers, to run around (a little) letting off steam, easing the frustrations of a normal working life.

The average weekend soccer player's competitive instinct can be satisfied more readily in an earthy challenge than in a battle of soccer wits.

They actually enjoy leaving their brains in the changing room and switching to automatic pilot. It is liberation.

They allow their hot pumping blood carry them through the highs and lows of a game, providing a physical outlet and release from mental strain, whilst saving their grey matter for the day job.

They don't want to be lumbered with even more obligations, responsibilities and restraints on their day off.

They want to **play soccer instinctively**, disengaging the mind and freeing themselves of the shackles of normal *cooperative* work and social duties.

The trouble is, only the very best of natural talents can play *instinctively* to any decent level.

It is **the manager's job to shackle them** again. *I'm not bossy; I just know what you should be doing*. They won't like that.

They will resent having a "hobby boss" and being bossed at all, in their spare time.

Many believe they are performing perfectly well already and see no need to adjust their own game. They can always blame the team's performance on other weaker teammates.

They do not see a link between your desired changes and improvement. They do not see how **all the small things done right, can add up to one big, good thing**. That is, creating or denying goal chances and ultimately achieving a favourable result.

If they think the small things don't matter, they should think back to recent close defeats.

Some players are bad players because they have bad ears. They don't listen.

Instruction, at best, will go in one ear and out the other; or at worst, be vehemently opposed.

They are usually too young and yet to see the bigger picture. They see a mass of individuals performing diverse, barely connected tasks with just good or bad natural abilities.

Players without adequate soccer knowledge, despite admirable technical and physical skills, will not be in the right positions or make the right moves in important attacking or defensive situations.

They will not read the game correctly to make the correct supporting or covering runs. They will believe that their game is adequate because they will make the best of these bad starting and finishing positions, through their competent individual attributes.

They do not understand that to the educated eye that sees all the isolated tasks connected, their lack of positional awareness and team movement stands out like a sore thumb.

It will be hard for you to impart your knowledge and for many of these types of player, their vision will only become clear, if at all, after very many more frustrating games or seasons.

With these players, you need to tie them down to certain areas and tasks, giving them set objectives in their play and limiting their freedom to act intuitively under the influence of their own, as yet, underdeveloped soccer brain.

This is obviously not the ideal for them or you, but if you let them run free they will not perform for the team as well as a restrained version of them might.

Give them a job to do and insist they stick to it.

Clear vision of the team game, joining the dots of the individual tasks, comes eventually through experience and is rarely present in raw talent.

Experience or *reading the game* is a gift acquired normally through many games and seasons.

A realisation that you have seen these standard situations, even in open play, countless times before; and with the advantage of déjà vu, the knowledge to do the percentage thing, the right thing, this time around.

Soccer knowledge is doing the same things every time and expecting the same result.

Thus, soccer knowledge at local-league level is predominantly the preserve of the soccer aged. It is something most of us get when the chance to use it, at our highest playing level, is lost. It can be fast-tracked if you are fortunate enough, through exposure to a much higher standard of soccer.

Hopefully, not oblivious to the hurdles and restrictions, into the training ground and dressing room walks the lower league-level manager.

Daunting as the task may be, there is still only one way to do it well. That is, wholeheartedly committed to your soccer values; and honestly.

Players will accept a lot, but rarely dishonesty, in your dealings with them.

This allows you plenty of scope to use your charm and political skills but favouritism, scapegoating and broken promises are a big no-no.

Aware of the challenges ahead, the manager must reign in his expectations or at least apply a conservative timeframe to their implementation.

Soccer is not a game of chess and players are not inanimate, disposable pieces. He must show the same patience and discipline he requires from his players.

The manager must have the courage, composure and perseverance to allow the players' time to improve and adopt a new way of playing. Explain clearly the purpose of some aspect of their game you wish to change and encourage their opinions on it.

They need to execute it and so need to be totally convinced by it, or it will not work. Tactics are meaningless unless you can get them inside the hearts and minds of the players.

The tactics or desired competitive edge must be within their abilities and utilise their strengths.

Do not play a high defensive line with slow defenders. Do not hit a lot of high balls into a striker who is a poor *header* of the ball. Do not have your fast striker coming short and your slower one staying long. Do not force a skilful penetrative winger to be a track-back tackler. Do not force a square peg into a round hole.

Weakness must be camouflaged, not exposed.

The manager has taken on a long-term project judged on short-term results.

The long-term mission is to get his team to employ enough of **a pass-and-move game through the correct team shape**, in order to dominate possession and create more goal opportunities than the opposition.

To have all players understand their positions, and the role of each position in the various ephemeral support triangles and team units.

To have all players appreciate the significance of each last third of the pitch and the **overriding importance of the goal area**, as opposed to all other areas of the pitch.

You won't go far in life or soccer if you don't know where the goalposts are.

To have all players understand set-plays and regularly to seek advantage through them.

The short-term objective is always this week's result. *Winning doesn't really matter...as long as you win.*

A manager must communicate well and stick to his theme of the day. A manager must be frugal with his technical advice on match day and avoid information overload.

He must fix one thing at a time, e.g. concentrate on shape and width, moving on to pass-and-move when they literally have the first concept up and running.

He must deal with each player or units separately, giving them information specific to their tasks or matched to their ability to comprehend, sparing them other details.

He must fix frequent events like set-plays separately, attacking throw-ins one week, defensive corners the next.

He should go back over forgotten or more likely unheeded advice regularly and as needs must.

Thus, it takes time, and only if time is taken will the lessons be learnt.

I would wish that a team of local-level players could read a book like this and instantly become a better team. But I know that is not realistic. It would be a bit like reading a "how to play golf" book and the next day playing single figure golf, off a 24-handicap.

The theory takes time to grind into practice.

Along with any necessary cultural changes, I would estimate a full season may pass with basically the same squad before enough of the theory shows in practice.

Reaping rewards the next season through improved or more easily gained results.

Learning and improving through repetition and practice, over time.

Success rarely comes easily. In the meantime, **sign some good players**.

You may not be able to sign them, but you will need to assess your own quickly if you are to succeed, either in improving them or replacing them before they replace you.

Look for *physical fitness, speed, technical ability, strength of character and tactical awareness.*

Do they score, create or prevent goals? Or do they link play well between those that prevent and those that create?

If they do none of these things, they are playing for the opposition.

Some players are quick, but don't play quick. They don't know when to use their speed, or they have a reactive rather than proactive game. Others seem to be a yard ahead all the time, not drawn to the ball but drawn to where the ball will be.

This is what is called "reading the game". Can you learn that? Yes.

If you pay attention to what you are watching, you will learn through experience that **the same things tend to happen in the same way**. This enables you to anticipate what is most likely to happen and get a head start on those that don't.

This is what reading the game is. It is not innate; it is achieved through practice and concentration. Good players have put in the practice and the concentration, naturally over the years, without a second thought. Bad players play each game like it's a new experience.

This is because they do not waste time thinking about what they have seen before and what they are seeing now. As manager, you have to draw their attention to what they are seeing and hope the learning curve can be shortened, through your advice.

Players may make mistakes, have dips in form and take time to learn something new, but *they can all learn*. Some just learn quicker than others.

I think we encourage players to choose a position too soon in their playing lives.

The South American way, or the way kids used to learn in the street, is that virtually everybody has the same position and all learn to attack, score goals and defend.

They gain an all-round skill set, only choosing or being allocated a position that most suits their style and physique when they have physically developed.

In local-level soccer, we may not play "total soccer", but all players, regardless of their positions, need to have a certain all-round skill level: able to attack and defend, and to think in an attack-minded or defensive fashion, depending on the game situation.

It is like signing a new player if you can discover a hidden ability in one of your squad; converting a defender to a forward and vice versa.

Look at your squad and see if someone has a perfect match in attributes for a task other than the one they are presently charged with.

It may solve a positional crisis for you or make use of an individual who is not performing in his original post, revitalising his game and this position.

Soccer is a team game. **Teamwork divides the effort and multiplies the effect**. Eleven linked individuals, forming chains of two, three and four links, breaking up to create different chains as the ball moves through other areas of the pitch.

Chains are only as strong as their weakest link. Meaning the players next to you need to support you, in attack and defence, or you will not be able to perform to your ability.

If I can make up some figures here: your team needs its players to be 80% team and just 20% individual-oriented. By this, I mean the playing instinct should significantly favour the team first and their own needs a clear second. *The name on the front of the jersey is more important than the name on the back.*

Some players are 80% individual, and are addicted to pursuing their own desires and agendas. Even if you have an excess of team-oriented "water carrier"-type players trying to make up for this, the team is unbalanced. You *need good individuals*, but with every one of these the team must come first.

Individualism, in excess, leads to conceded possession, lost opportunities and lost games.

It is not always somebody dribbling too much or not passing. It can manifest itself as playing within oneself, giving up too easily, not supporting and not pushing themselves for the good of the team. It is also often seen in the player who gets sent off or commits a selfish foul when you least need it.

Such players work, generally unknowingly, against the team's spirit and positive motivation.

As soon as the athletic ability of this 80% individual-oriented-type begins to diminish, which happens quicker and quicker in the lower levels, they are of no use, as their team ability has not been developed. Their team awareness is still in its infancy.

Players bring their individual characters out with them onto the playing field.

There are players who tend to disappoint on the big occasions; players that shine regularly against weak opposition and yet freeze in a tough match.

Players who let you down on the pitch will let you down off it, in the same type of way. This is nothing to do with soccer ability.

Put another way, their same personal faults off-pitch will manifest themselves on it.

For example, weak anger and emotional management, bad nutrition or personal fitness, bad concentration and inattentiveness, reckless behaviour, lack of confidence, nervousness, selfishness, laziness... and the list could go on and on.

People also have good characteristics or attributes that generally compensate; however, *when the going gets tough, their currently prevailing character trait will shine through.*

If you watch and/or play long enough with certain players, you can know many aspects of their off-field persona by their on-field behaviour. Or if you get to know somebody off the pitch first, you can usually read their soccer style and attitude in advance of seeing it.

Having some bad character attributes does not necessarily mean they will be bad for the team. We all (probably) have some bad attributes in our make-ups.

It is the manager's job to learn these and cope with them in a team context. For example, having a petulant prima donna winger is a totally different thing to having a petulant prima donna centre half.

A bully in midfield, a psychopathic studs-down-the-back-of-your-calf full back, a cheating centre forward are not always a bad thing.

A silent assassin, who seems to hurt the opposition whilst never doing very much else for you, and a constant moaner who plays mainly with his mouth and winds up your own team as much as the opposition, can all help in certain matches.

However, you rarely control them; they control you. They are unpredictable, likely to get sent off or gift opportunity to the opposition, *the higher the stakes get.*

You will spend an inordinate amount of time trying to contain their worst excesses, trying to bend these traits to the team's advantage.

Mostly though, you will overlook them, because of their other soccer skills and capabilities, or their place in the club hierarchy. Politics is everywhere.

Worse than the on-the-pitch occasional disruptive demeanour, is the often concealed but pervasive negative influence on the training ground, in the changing room or in the bar.

It is the rotten apple in the barrel. This is not usually a good player, but often a good player's mate. *Management is the art of keeping apart those that don't like you and those that haven't yet made up their minds.*

Give me eleven men, strong and true, any day. If you can manage to change the culture and bring in a pure soccer ethic, there will be no room in your team for weak links and rotten apples. In the meantime, cultivate a thick skin and control them as best you can.

Patient, gradual change is for the long term.

The short term is all about match tactics and the proverbial "taking each game as it comes".

So set up your team to achieve an optimal result from the players you have on a given day. Adapt your playing style to match or dictate events in real game time.

I like to use 4-4-2 at lower level, as it is easily understood. Players understand their roles in it and find it hard to hide. It can easily become 4-5-1 or 4-2-3-1 during open play and, in fact, these seem to be the current professional versions of it.

I certainly don't get bogged down in formations, as they are just default starting positions which ensure a solid spine and a springboard for width.

Good players will generally be in the right place when they are needed anyway. The shape is just their launch pad to make runs from or their allocated range to protect.

The real battle is won and lost by the quality of the communication, cooperation and the pass-and-move combinations within the team's units.

Pre-match Warm-up

I am not a great believer in meeting too early at a pitch, if there is no reason to do so. In the lower levels, with the standard of facilities, meeting early can be more depressing than it is worthwhile. One hour before is the aim, with the definite proviso that all players must be out on the pitch to start the official warm up 30 minutes before kickoff.

They should warm up gradually by running: **a warm-up that promotes the mobility of joints and the flexibility of muscle**. Jog, joint rotation, jog with side-to-sides etc, stretch and flex, jog with sprints, ball work, and fast feet drills using cones and bibs.

They should all reach top speed at some point in the warm-up. The first full sprint and recovery should not be left for the match. This can all be done in 20 minutes.

After the team chat and a couple of minutes before kickoff, the players should be doing their own individual jogging, stretching, jumping and short sprints to get themselves quickly back to their warmed-up state and match ready.

During the hour before the match, a lot of individual talks and motivation can be going on in the background. The manager, assistant and coaches work on this the whole hour before kickoff.

Pre-match Address

Your instructions before the match may point players to the theory of what they are trying to do and their connectedness in the team structure. They are not alone. **We are all in this together**.

Offer a *brief* résumé of the big picture and advice targeted at the receiver. Individuals with different abilities and varying temperaments require differing technical counsel and motivational approaches.

You should get this over to them individually, in units and as a team. This can go on long before the final dressing room en masse, motivational send-off: previously at training, in the car on the way, whilst getting changed and during the warm-up.

The actual final chat should not take more than 10 minutes, as if they don't know at this stage what they are supposed to be doing, it is too late.

Any long-winded tactical explanation is a waste of breath; and if it is sprung on them or they don't fully understand it, it will probably be detrimental to a fragile confidence.

Confidence and the lack of it are contagious.

Goalkeeping, goal scoring and ball carrying are all confidence-draining activities. Goalkeeper, centre forward, wingers and playmaker will **need constant reassurance**.

You won't make all the points below, but the players should go out with these in the recesses of their minds; because in the hours, days and weeks prior to this moment you have been grinding into them just such advice and instruction.

Your communication can now be short and direct, as a few *key words or a statement* will imply the lessons behind all the previous coaching and remind the players to heed them.

You should calm the goalkeeper. A cool head doesn't get caught in no man's land. Ask him to **concentrate at all times** the ball is in his half.

Pay special attention to his decision-making and footwork, and to talk and listen to his defence. **The goal is your baby**. **Protect it above all else**.

You may address the centre halves together, advising them to cover for each other, to communicate and synchronise their actions. **Safety first**, especially early on.

Ball watching is the enemy of good defending, all over the pitch.

Pass people on, rather than allow yourself to be dragged out of position.

Do not squeeze your opposition forwards onto your own midfield when these have possession. Rather, drop back and provide a safe out-ball.

Do not play too high a line, but rather be ready to side/backpedal as the opposition's forward pass is made.

Stay touch-tight in the box. Start marking from nearest to the goal, swapping opponents if you have to. Stay on your feet unless you are absolutely sure of the tackle.

The goal is your baby. Protect it above all else.

Address the midfield. Advise them to **hunt in packs**. That is, squeeze together when seeking to dispossess the opposition, not singularly.

Make sure they have their man marked tight in the defending last third.

They should be careful not to get too close to each other on the ball, but to support each other.

Distribute the ball cautiously and in a timely manner, feeding the wings and forwards.

Get their heads up and think. One of them has to be in a central position at all times.

One of them has to get to the box if a cross is coming in. **Have shots, if the ball falls within range**. Be a little more adventurous with the distribution in the attacking last third.

Make sure the full backs and the wingers work as a unit, with the full back following the winger up the pitch as his back-up and safe out-pass.

The full back must follow the instruction and lead of the centre halves in all defensive matters.

The winger should get his cross over quickly, once in the attacking last third; otherwise, practising good movement and ball maintenance until he gets there.

Especially take advantage of any penetration he has made, by looking at the damage in the opposition ranks behind him and playing the ball inside, into that damaged area.

The winger is to defend the opposition full back, and to receive and follow defensive advice from his full back and captain.

Does the winger come back into the defending last third every time? Or do you want him, when he reads it right, to stay available on the edge of the defensive last third, ready to launch a counter attack...

Encourage the forwards to be clever and sharp, and combine their runs.

To **be proactive not reactive** in their movement.

To **attack the ball in the box** and not to be shy in having a shot.

To believe in themselves, that the ball is coming to them and that they will score.

On a team basis, briefly outline the shape, pass-and-*MOVE* and the **importance of the last third areas**, where everything is heightened and the game is won and lost.

Remind players that **they only have their own job to do** and not to wander easily from it.

Remind them that the **little things matter**:

Get a throw-in instead of losing the ball.

Get a corner when in a good position but under pressure.

Sense that the passing is getting tight, and know when to apply the big switch and clear it out of that area.

Don't foul just because the opposition invites you to.

Stay on your feet; don't get beat.

Clear the ball towards corner flags to give your forwards a chance, instead of kicking it back through the middle to the opponent keeper.

Kick it off the park for a throw-in deep in their half, rather than risk losing possession in your half when you have no option for a pass and everything else is risky.

The above are all generalisations, a five-minute reheat of much of the advice from previous chapters. Advice that is constant and relevant to every game and hopefully imbedded into your players by now. **A picture that can be recreated in their minds by a few key words**.

Your team set-up and strategy will focus on the opposition in hand.

If you know the opposition, you may have some individual advice to combat certain known threats or increase opportunities. This may already have influenced your team selection. Players need to know what the team is going out to do. Are we playing cautiously in the first half? Are we free to go for the result straight from kickoff?

Patience is a virtue in a manager. You might set up to be solid behind the ball, attacking conservatively; making sure the strong compact shape in the middle is never compromised by keeping both midfielders deep and central, as counter-attack insurance.

Wait 45 minutes. Wait 60 minutes. **It is not a race**. Frustrate the opposition into causing their own defeat. Sometimes, just by sitting back and waiting for the counter, the opponents will gift you a goal or two by mistakes or reckless attacking.

Thirty minutes is a long time to do damage and act recklessly, if needs must.

Sometimes, **before you can win the game you have to not lose it**.

You may want to commit to the attack from the start and catch them cold. Starting quickly is often best and is an easier mindset to induce.

Encourage your wingers to push up, supported by the full backs, bringing the game to the opposition. Control the game later from a position of dominance.

If you manage to come in at half-time a couple of goals up, you can always play more defensively in the second half. These are the basic, tried and tested **plan A and plan B of local-level soccer**.

Your players, eventually through experience, should **have a controlled defensive and a controlled attacking system** in their repertoire and be able to switch from one to the other, as necessary, during a game.

One team set-up might be strong through the spine at all times, with a restraint on getting caught forward for full backs and midfielders. This may concede possession in certain areas, but aims at frustrating a team of known superior standing.

Another set-up may offer more freedom to attack, whilst maintaining shape and work rate. This would be my standard set-up when playing against similar or inferior opposition.

All-out defence or attack are different set-ups entirely. These are usually learnt on the job and are a natural, late response to the endgame situation.

These are versions of defending the Alamo at one end or laying siege to Troy at the other. They are **built on improvisation, individual spirit and talent**, with one side parking the team bus on the edge of their 18-yard box, whilst the other side systematically trashes it.

Ultimately, it is all about players, but systems do upset teams and affect the result.

Give them something concrete to go out and achieve. **Give them purpose**.

Warn about personal discipline and how free kicks and cards damage the side.

The last minute or so is usually taken up by motivational-type clichés, often led by the players themselves. These should ensure that the players are up for it and ready from the first whistle, but are not going out there wanting to assault people.

The team should stride the pitch with the swagger of a confident, winning side.

If you need any tips on that, search online for "man management" or "sports psychology"!

In my experience, local league-level players can concentrate for about 20 minutes before mental fatigue sets in. The break at half-time may give you another limited period of team focus. Incidences in the game may temporarily restore or lower this concentration.

If players can get into the right shape and create movement and, therefore, opportunities in these lucid periods, it may be enough to secure a result. They can coast easier on automatic pilot once they have started out in the right fashion.

After the inevitable concentration collapse, your instructions should be on an individual basis. These will concern the separate battles that have arisen between opposing players in important areas of the pitch.

Renewed motivation and regeneration, through substitutions and position changes, will be your main weapon now.

Each match scenario calls for distinct managerial input at different times during the game.

Every match situation you will ever see has happened before or is a variation, so we are not reinventing the wheel here. The matches we play in, or manage, after reaching a certain critical number, are versions of games we have been involved in before.

If only we could remember what the outcome and analysis of them was, so that this time we could analyse and respond during the match. Fortunately, a good soccer brain does this automatically and calls it "reading the game" or experience.

I have noted a few standard managerial ploys, fixes and responses used in a few standard match scenarios.

I briefly touch on a couple of winning situations, but focus more on a *losing-the-match* scenario, on the basis that **if it's not broken, don't fix it**.

Do not fall into the trap of if it's not broken, fix it until it is.

This does not mean judge the state of the game only by its current result. **If the tide has turned against you, you need to recognise this and act before it is too late**.

If you are easily winning, with *no sign of a comeback* at any point in the game, your tactical job is done. The hard work was all done in training. Nurse and encourage your side to play keep-ball and practise their movement for a future harder match.

Lean back and enjoy, and look forward to the full-time whistle. Use your subs in an innocuous or defensive fashion, giving the subs a run out and saving the legs of others.

If you are narrowly winning late on, you may wish to hang on to what you have. Change your formation and playing mode to your known defensive set-up: 4-5-1 or 4-1-4-1.

Make sure the defence does not react by dropping deep, too early. They must stick to defending the last third and then the 18-yard box as normal, ruthlessly squeezing the ball and moving out as soon as the ball is cleared.

Do drop your wingers and central midfielders deeper, putting your first concerted squeeze on the opposition as they pass the halfway line.

In possession, play the ball mainly on the wings, eating up time with throw-ins and scrappy bogged-down play. Put it into the opposition-half corner-flag area and move up behind it in a controlled fashion.

First half

You send the team out full of the theory, and with the willingness and motivation to pursue it.

This works, nearly works or fails. If it works, carry on. If it nearly works, in that you are not seriously losing, then carry on.

If you have shipped a couple of goals without reply, it may be time to respond.

You need to identify the problem and the likelihood of it recurring. If a winger or forward is terrorising you, switch his marker, double-up on him or identify and cut off his supply.

If somebody is having a nightmare in a defensive position, consider dropping someone in beside him to help. You may need to reemphasise (shout) "**touch-tight in the box**".

If your defence players are going through a shaky patch, encourage them to clear their lines for a while; try to find corner flags, rather than midfielders, with their passes.

If you are losing centre midfield, you can drop a forward back to occupy their holding midfielder. Now you are playing 4-5-1 or 4-1-3-1-1, if we want to be pedantic...and why should I change now this far into the book!

You may need to do this and other emergency defensive measures, to prevent any more goals going in before the half-time respite, when a more advanced response can be devised.

If your wingers are not in the game or are getting short shrift, you can encourage them, lift their confidence, get them to swap wings. You can encourage your midfield to find them earlier and your wingers to be more creative in their movement.

This, I am afraid, entails shouting and gesturing from your box, showing your players that you are not happy and badgering them into concentrating, running and competing more effectively.

Having made any emergency fixes that you can, hopefully plugging the gaps for a while, you need to be thinking about how you are going to manage this situation at half-time.

How you are going to stop the rot and retrieve the deficit. More relevantly, how you are going to send your team back out there, confident that they can do so.

Individually, **players only have the actual ball for a very short period. The rest of their game is about decision-making**. Who should I mark? Where should I cover? Who should I support? What runs should I make?

Their apparently unsuccessful first-half answers to these decisional dilemmas may pinpoint the problem.

You may also have witnessed the revival of bad habits in certain players which, as we know, die hard.

Over-dribbling, slow or casual passing, standing off instead of closing down, bad and foul tackling, needlessly losing possession by consistently trying the hardest pass or refusing to get their heads up. Not tracking back, being immobile and hard to pass to.

You will need a notepad if you have that many problems.

Identify the most damaging traits and try to fix them.

Soccer is a simple game.

The answers to the team's problems will be simple.

However, a bit like the remedy for being overweight, **eat less**, **move more**, they will be hard to implement and enforce.

Half-time

I like to get the players in; let them get a gulp of energy drink (adios sugary tea and orange-eighths) and have a minute or so where nothing is said about the game situation.

Players should **compose themselves**, **calm down** if necessary; and all of us can have a little personal reflection on what has just happened and our part in it. It helps you get your managerial act together as well.

I might even ask them to pipe down and have a silent, critical look back at their own performance in that 45. Just a little thought on what they might have done differently, whilst they get some rest and rehydration.

If you are going to criticise someone, it's often better if they are sitting down and calm.

Other managers may like to get at the players as soon as they can, striking while the iron is hot. I have no particular criticism of this; it is just not for me.

If the on-pitch problems of the first half are clear to you; if you have made up your mind about the solutions, what you are going to say and any tactical changes you are going to make, you should **get their attention and start talking**.

Some call it ranting; I call it motivational speaking.

For example, if you have been punished by crosses, make sure the full back and winger are getting tighter and preventing them. If players have been unmarked in the box, reprimand your centre halves into concentrating, communicating more and marking closer.

If people have been allowed shoot from around the box, the central defence and midfield need to tighten up on that, by closing down without overly committing and getting beaten.

If the opposition has too much good possession in your half, you may need to drop back sooner, in numbers, and as soon as possession is lost; compacting the central area, then squeezing more effectively in units.

In possession, you may clear your lines earlier, choosing to compete and start play in their half until you have composed yourselves.

Giving away too many dead-ball situations that have caused problems can be solved by cutting out the unnecessary free-kicks and panicky clearances.

These are often the result of **sudden ball loss caused by a lack of options on the ball**. This can lead to a lack of support for the first defender, who is then pressured into an individual mistake. **Support the man on the ball and the first defender**.

If we are not creating, then you can bet it is the movement that is at fault. It is probably, sluggish, mistimed, uncoordinated or nonexistent. "Predictable" would be the catch-all term and end result. The answer is to **think** and *move* **more** or *move* **better**.

Are we overplaying the ball in tight situations and getting caught? Or losing possession in the attacking last third before creating goal chances?

The **big switch** and expanding out instead of contracting in, when in tight situations, are the tactics here. We may need to be more direct, **putting the ball sooner into the opponent's last third and 18-yard box**.

Give our forwards and attacking midfielders something positive to chase and attack, in and around the 18-yard box where the goals come from.

You quickly assess and deal with the problems of the past half, to hopefully prevent them reoccurring or at least lessen their impact on the next half.

Sometimes it is not clear what exactly the problem is; and in this case you need to tease out the problem and thereby, hopefully, the solution from the players.

Or, if there are a lot of problems, you have to ascertain which one is the catalyst and which ones are just symptoms or consequences of the principal fault.

As managers, we do sometimes kid ourselves as to how much influence we wield during a match. We do have a few tools, but though *we kick and head every ball*, our fate is firmly in the hands of our players.

Our main influence is almost all pre-match and in the background.

The match-day tools we have are individual and team psychological motivation, substitutions and positional changes.

Tactical changes, such as favouring one style of play.

Loading different areas of the pitch. Changing team shape. Swapping player's positions.

Being *more* or *less* direct in our play.

Committing more resources to attack or setting up more defensively.

All of these, apart from being physical responses, can have a less visible but tangible positive psychological effect on your own team and a negative one on the opposition.

For this effect alone **it is worth shaking things up**, **in a losing situation**.

It can be a psychological blow for a player to be taken off at half-time. If he has been really poor, "you started badly and got worse", it may be necessary to do so.

If you feel no amount of covering up or encouragement will improve his performance, and for the good of the team and the result, the position needs to be improved right now.

"Warm up, you're coming off!"

A good manager is prepared to make the tough decisions when it would be more convenient for him to ignore them. The easy decisions make themselves.

At local-league level and in a club without a culture of self-discipline, you may need to cushion this blow, if you want the player there, fully committed, next week.

You can couch this as a tactical ploy, in view of the desperate situation, necessitating the sacrificing of his position if it is to work.

You can take a centre half off, telling him we are soon going to play three at the back, that his substitute is eventually going to push up and play holding-midfield.

The real effect being you have swapped centre halves.

You can take a forward off, proposing to play one up front and to put his replacement in attacking-midfield. You can then switch someone up front with either your next substitution or simply by ordering an on-pitch reshuffle. End effect: a change in forward.

Unless the player is really thin-skinned, the tactical switch is more likely to be presented genuinely and the player removed from play should be strong enough to get over this ignominy.

What I am really saying is that individuals at half-time should not be overly criticised in front of others. Try to select a unit to direct criticism at, e.g. central midfield or the back four.

You could criticise the whole midfield for letting the opposition play around them and/or for not being aggressive enough. You could have a go at the central-defensive pairing for not covering each other or communicating well enough.

Players can and should be criticised, but the **criticism should be constructive**.

"You played that pass before you were ready; take a touch, get your head up and relax."

Not: "that was a f***ing terrible pass, do that again you **** and you're off."

Players need to believe that they are in control and can fix anything they are doing wrong.

Better still, you don't go on about what they have done badly, but approach it more positively.

You could ask a full back to get closer to their winger in the last third and concentrate on sending him outside, rather than highlight the fact that he has cost a goal by letting him drive goal-wards.

Suggest that your forwards who have hardly had a kick concentrate more on their movement; versions of "let's see how mobile these centre halves really are", rather than "you have been marked right out of the game". **Say NO to negativity**.

You may need to remove two players at half-time if the situation demands it; seldom three, as it is always advisable to hold one back until later, not least as insurance against injury. *Keep a fresh pair of legs up your sleeve.*

You may decide to hold the substitutions for 10 or 15 minutes, to see if attitude or performance levels have changed.

In this case, you may *subtly* threaten substitutions by having the subs warm up and telling all that you expect them to come out flying and give you a good 15 minutes, as if it was their last.

You have now analysed the past defensive faults and taken steps to rectify them. You have noted the team's creative failings and suggested improvements.

You have implied there will be future measures and personnel changes, should these steps not take effect. You have shown them you are unhappy, but are not going to cry over spilt milk.

Now you need to send them back out, lifted, reanimated and confident that their bad half is behind them, and that the next bad half will be the opposition's.

Challenge them to go out and win the half and hopefully the game. Do they want to lose like mice or men?

"Surely you can score against these?"

To the midfielders: "Do you think you can stop their number 10 playing this half? Make sure you feed the left winger this half."

To a central defensive unit: "No more goals against and we will win this."

To a winger: "I want at least four crosses from you in this half."

To a forward: "Make sure you are clever enough to get on the end of something in their box."

Again, **give them something concrete to go out and achieve**. Give them purpose.

This is where your assistant manager, your captain and any other skilled motivational speaker in the dressing room might chip in to help.

So long as this is positive and uplifting, it will bond the team, give them all a feeling of personal investment in the upcoming 45 minutes, and a shared commitment to reversing the result.

You will hopefully send them out with a positive attitude, which can be doubly effective since they presumably came in with a negative one.

This can give you a psychological edge on the opposition as the second half begins.

I once played in the FA Cup first round at Swindon for March Town, a small non-league club. Swindon Town had kick-off to start the first half.

Just seconds before the kick-off, two or three of their players casually moved up towards their left-wing halfway line, joining the winger already there.

The kick was taken and went back to one of their centre halves. Our forward players moved up field, to close him down.

Swindon's by now four left wingers charged down onto our right back, and their centre half floated a lovely long ball right over his head.

He struggled to win this ball, just managing to get it out for a throw-in, which they promptly took. And having so many players in this area, they contrived to immediately get a shot on target from the edge of our box.

Our keeper made a great save, tipping it over the bar for a corner. Which again, they promptly took, forcing our goalie to make another great save, which produced another corner.

We had hardly touched the ball. Seconds that felt like minutes had passed and seemingly through no fault of our own, we had conceded two attempts on target and two corners.

My own first touch involved trying to keep a ball in on the wing, only to be kicked into touch, ball and all, by a Chris Kamara *fair* tackle. This was accompanied by an intimidating, approving roar from the crowd.

The shock of their opening 90-miles-an-hour gambit and deliberate ploy of going directly for the minnow's jugular had caught us cold. You might expect that type of mass forced attack in the last five minutes but not in the first few.

We were soon enough 2-0 down. It remained so at the end, but we never really recovered psychologically to believe in winning. We were as good as beaten with the game hardly started.

Substitutions, tactical switches and motivational speeches can have a similar psychological effect; and if a team starts badly in either half, it can be a shock they don't recover from.

Aim to **recover from a bad first half, from the very first moment of the second**. The opposition may come out expecting more of the same. They may therefore be complacent and temporarily vulnerable. **Really up the tempo** for the next 15 minutes.

Second half

I believe in change, especially if the game is not going your way. Change is good for change's sake. Even if the value of a change or substitution is not exactly clear to your players, it can have a lifting effect on their spirits.

If they believe something has happened and now things are different, it can wake them up and give them new impetus. When you do nothing, a certain feeling of inevitability and resignation can sink into your players.

Your aim has to be to make it uncomfortable for the opposition. Don't give them what they want to defend or what they were happy with; **give them something different**, hopefully something they don't like.

You may have sent them out to start the second half in a different team shape. 3-4-3 can be the way to chase a substantial deficit and can take the game to the opposition; that is, ensure the game is played a little more in their half than in yours.

You cannot now maintain possession and play out from the back so easily, and the defence is forced to be more direct with its passes, hitting the forwards sooner than in the first half.

You should keep one of the quicker full backs next to the two centre halves; or take off a centre half and tuck your two full backs into the middle.

In this set up, you might substitute your least mobile or ball-friendly defender.

This means that if the opposition attack up your wing, into your defending last third, one of three players acts as the regular full back and the other two mark in the centre.

You have, in effect, sacrificed a full-back position for one up front. The three at the back now, with help further up the pitch from the wingers, discharge both full-back duties.

During possession and when combating a central opposition move, they all play in the middle, protecting the direct route to their goal, forcing the opposition attacks out to the wings. The three need to raise their game now. They have no choice.

This is a strong defence centrally, where it really matters.

You now need to get the ball into their last third quicker than you may have previously. You have more numbers available up there now and less at the back. Therefore, it suits you to start playing the ball in their half and being more direct.

A team can only concentrate for so long before they slip back into automatic pilot. If your players' automatic pilot is still at novice level, then **they need to take advantage in these enlightened periods**.

They should go hell-for-leather in the next 15 minutes; with **high-pressure defending on any opposition possession**, attempting to keep play high up the pitch.

Your team should jump on the opponents in packs as soon as the ball is lost, working that much harder to offer support and movement for the man in possession.

They can attack the ball with more gusto than previously; of course, with impeccable timing.

The three strikers will have more chances to create space on the wings by interchanging runs. They will be able to link up more easily with the winger to create crossing opportunities in the attacking third, whilst still having at least two forwards in the box to meet them.

They should come out of the dressing room on an immediate mission to turn things around. Whilst your team can still focus and before the opposition can react through substitution or tactical change, you may catch them off-guard.

The opponents may be unprepared and expecting the same "lose mentality" team they sent into the dressing room.

Goals change games. If you get one, your opponents may get nervous; and their confidence could begin to evaporate and condense into your team.

Even if you don't manage to redress the score-line in this period, the psychological balance may have shifted in your favour for the remaining 20 or 30 minutes.

This can manifest itself as the winning team sitting back deeper and earlier than recommended, defending their lead.

Obviously, one could write any losing match scenario and fix it with tactical manoeuvrings and substitutions on paper. Unfortunately, the real game happens on grass.

Soccer is an amazingly unpredictable game. We have all, no doubt, seen and been part of great comebacks and collapses from the most unlikely of positions.

They are not the norm, but they do happen frequently enough to be a massive and exciting part of the game. There is usually a catalyst to the collapse and comeback, such as a substitution or tactical switch, injury, freak or exceptional goal, penalty kick or sending-off.

During the game, managers are dependent on their players to get the right result but that does not mean we cannot give them a boost along the way.

Using our imagination, experience and positivity we can stimulate them into nursing a comfortable win or making an inspired comeback.

We have to believe that just as much as we expect them to.

On the other hand, you could do nothing, make no changes and that might work. It's a funny old game...it's just not supposed to be.

The three substitutions allowed normally follow a pattern: they arrive after an hour, after 70 and after 85 minutes.

Depending on how the game is going, these can be brought forward or set back five minutes or so.

Fresh legs and a desire to impress can revive a flagging team.

Some players are natural impact performers. Late in a game, when it is more open and presumably slower-paced, is a perfect stage for them.

The kitchen sink is usually only thrown at a result in the last five minutes.

In a Cup game, when you are not worried about the goals against balance, all-out attack may be declared earlier.

The attitude should be, **we do not lose the game, we just run out of time**.

In this case, you will put your ball-winning centre half up front and leave just two speedy players as your defence.

You will enforce a high line and the goalkeeper will play as a safe, out-pass defender and sweeper.

Now you have to keep the ball in the opponent's half and preferably last third.

Bang it into their 18-yard box at every opportunity, pouncing on the opposition every time they might get hold of it.

It takes a brave winning team to call your bluff, leaving strikers up front and not dropping everybody deep.

This tactic is most effective when you are only trailing by one or two goals, as the opposition are much more nervous and conservative with such a narrow lead.

That is why I believe that **one goal is never enough**. You put that in your pocket and carry on looking for another. One goal up in the last 10 minutes is never a comfortable ride. I would **only blatantly defend it in injury time**.

If you manage to win, everybody will be happy; your night, your week and training sessions will come easy.

If you lose, I find it unproductive to immediately or overly lambast your team and players. **You should have motivated them before or during the match**. It's too late now.

In the heat of the moment, it is very hard to have a refined analysis of what went wrong.

Even if you do, it is unlikely that the team see it that way yet; and attacking individuals in such an atmosphere can undo a lot of the team bonding achieved earlier and destroy confidence.

The players need to retain some pride and, if they are any good, will secretly be their own worst critics when they think back. Your withering or dejected look can say enough.

Give the team a general critique about the number of mistakes, the lack of quality, effort or concentration, without citing incidences or naming and shaming.

Ask them to go away and think about it and their performance, and that you will talk about it in midweek or before the next match. Sleep on it.

You need to pick yourself and your team up during the week.

You need to have analysed what went wrong and have quiet words with those responsible to try and prevent it occurring again.

For every team, a season always comes down to a couple of important games, whether in winning leagues or Cups, chasing promotion or fighting relegation. Even those in mid-table nothingness have a couple of season-defining games.

A good Cup run, an unexpected victory or just a great performance can lift the spirits; and at the right time in the right match, your season changes, people smile and your job is secure.

Not that anybody else necessarily wants it.

We are not robots. The theory will never be superior to the individuals trying to implement it.

Players will still hit bad passes, make bad runs, and ignore soccer theory — in particular, pass-and-move, because it is a sharp and fit theory, not a dull and lazy one.

That doesn't mean the theory isn't right, even for our level. It means that it is a nonstop lesson, full of repeats and setbacks; but by pursuing it, you might capture some of it and get your rewards on local-level match day.

At local-league level, we do not need to implement all of it, or for the entire match. The basics alone should be enough to give you a competitive edge.

Soccer theory is a percentage game.

Good players will embody the theory naturally and instinctively, without needing it analysed or written down. But nobody fails at it. They just find their level.

The book is over. The key message must be keep your shape, work hard, encourage movement, confidence and character.

In soccer, as in life, you get what you deserve, *most of the time*.

Soccer is about people and it reflects life.

Life with all its ups and downs, joys and frustrations, rewards and disappointments.

Learn to win. Accept a loss. Win fair. Lose graciously. Move on. There is always next weekend.

About the Author

Paul Hutchinson lives in Dublin, Ireland. You can contact Paul at:

thesoccerhutch@gmail.com